HOT TOPICS

By Jennifer Lombardo

Portions of this book originally appeared in *Online Social Networking* by Carla Mooney.

Published in 2017 by
Lucent Press, an Imprint of Greenhaven Publishing, LLC
353 3rd Avenue
Suite 255
New York, NY 10010

Designer: Andrea Davison-Bartolotta
Editor: Jennifer Lombardo

Cataloging-in-Publication Data

Names: Lombardo, Jennifer.
Title: Social networking: staying safe in the online world / Jennifer Lombardo.
Description: New York : Lucent Press, 2017. | Series: Hot Topics | Includes index.
Identifiers: ISBN 9781534560215 (library bound) | ISBN 9781534560222 (ebook)
Subjects: LCSH: Online social networks–Juvenile literature. | Social networks–Juvenile literature. | Online social networks–Safety measures–Juvenile literature. | Internet–Safety measures--Juvenile literature.
Classification: LCC HM742.L66 2017 | DDC 302.3–dc23

Printed in the United States of America

CPSIA compliance information: Batch #CW17KL: For further information contact Greenhaven Publishing LLC, New York, New York at 1-844-317-7404.

Please visit our website, www.greenhavenpublishing.com. For a free color catalog of all our high-quality books, call toll free 1-844-317-7404 or fax 1-844-317-7405.

CONTENTS

FOREWORD

Adolescence is a time when many people begin to take notice of the world around them. News channels, blogs, and talk radio shows are constantly promoting one view or another; very few are unbiased. Young people also hear conflicting information from parents, friends, teachers, and acquaintances. Often, they will hear only one side of an issue or be given flawed information. People who are trying to support a particular viewpoint may cite inaccurate facts and statistics on their blogs, and news programs present many conflicting views of important issues in our society. In a world where it seems everyone has a platform to share their thoughts, it can be difficult to find unbiased, accurate information about important issues.

It is not only facts that are important. In blog posts, in comments on online videos, and on talk shows, people will share opinions that are not necessarily true or false, but can still have a strong impact. For example, many young people struggle with their body image. Seeing or hearing negative comments about particular body types online can have a huge effect on the way someone views himself or herself and may lead to depression and anxiety. Although it is important not to keep information hidden from young people under the guise of protecting them, it is equally important to offer encouragement on issues that affect their mental health.

The titles in the Hot Topics series provide readers with different viewpoints on important issues in today's society. Many of these issues, such as teen pregnancy and Internet safety, are of immediate concern to young people. This series aims to give readers factual context on these crucial topics in a way that lets them form their own opinions. The facts presented throughout also serve to empower readers to help themselves or support people they know who are struggling with many of the challenges adolescents face today. Although negative viewpoints are not ignored or downplayed, this series allows young people to see that the challenges they face are not insurmountable. Eating disorders can be overcome, the Internet can be navigated safely, and pregnant teens do not have to feel hopeless.

Quotes encompassing all viewpoints are presented and cited so readers can trace them back to their original source, verifying for themselves whether the information comes from a reputable place. Additional books and websites are listed, giving readers a starting point from which to continue their own research. Chapter questions encourage discussion, allowing young people to hear and understand their classmates' points of view as they further solidify their own. Full-color photographs and enlightening charts provide a deeper understanding of the topics at hand. All of these features augment the informative text, helping young people understand the world they live in and formulate their own opinions concerning the best way they can improve it.

Social Networking: An Overview

For someone who has grown up in the technology age, it can be hard to imagine a time before computers connected the world. The Internet, once used only by world governments, eventually developed into the massive information system people use every day. It became popular in private homes in 1991, but its rise in popularity was slow because most people did not know or understand what it could do. In 1997, the first social networking website was created, and since then, the use of online social networking has grown to become part of people's everyday lives.

Originally, the only people who could be on social networking websites were those who could afford a computer. However, cost is no longer a barrier to social network use. Computers and Internet access are more affordable than ever. Libraries offer free portals to the online world. Smartphones with monthly data plans are still relatively expensive, but their prices are dropping every year. Geographic barriers have also fallen. It is easy and inexpensive to chat online with friends almost anywhere in the world.

The introduction of multimedia capabilities to social networking sites has made them increasingly popular. For the first time in history, the average Internet user can upload pictures, music, and videos to web pages with ease. With these new tools, users can creatively express themselves online as never before. Displays of art, music, and writing abound on social networking websites, each one unique to its creator.

Young people are not the only ones who engage in online social networking. The adult world has also embraced social networking. Businesses, politicians, schools, libraries, and activists

Libraries offer free Internet use, so even people who cannot afford a computer or smartphone can have social media profiles.

have discovered the power of social networks to change the way they work. Websites that were once limited to young adults have now become popular with people of all ages. In fact, it is rare to find that a person or business does not have at least one social media account.

Many people believe that the growing use of social networks has had a positive impact on society. Worldwide networks introduce new ideas and cultures to a widening audience. Collaboration and cooperation across groups and countries is easier than ever. Some people argue, however, that too much time in front of a computer keyboard will have a negative impact. They question whether young people will develop adequate face-to-face communication skills. Others point out that as people feel less inhibited behind a computer screen, they may be more likely to participate in cyberbullying. Additionally, scammers and predators are able to use the Internet to target people for money or sexual interactions.

In recent years, the media spotlight on social networking has brought some complex issues to the forefront. All communities, whether online or offline, have a darker side and must deal with safety. Social networks are no exception. Dangers, such as predators, drugs, and pornography, lurk online. Countless cases of young people being lured by these elements abound in the news. Predators target teens on message boards and convince them to meet offline. Students link up with drug dealers through social network friends to buy drugs. Teens stumble onto

Posting pictures online that include drugs, alcohol, or other illegal activities can negatively impact a young adult's future.

pornographic pictures by following a link on a new friend's social network profile.

The ease with which users can run into trouble online concerns many adults. Some parents, schools, and legislators have called for the banning of these sites. "I talk to parents all the time about the need to educate themselves," said Ron Wenkart, general counsel for the Orange County Department of Education. "If they knew what their kids were up to, many of them would be horrified."[1] Other groups protest that banning is rarely effective. Instead, they believe adults have a responsibility to educate young people about social networking safety.

Another concern is the erosion of personal privacy as more information lands online. As people post their inner thoughts for the world to see, some people are very concerned by this abandonment of privacy. With teachers, colleges, and employers looking online, users may risk their reputations and futures over a few pictures of partying with friends. High school teacher Tom Goldsbury believes that students do not fully understand the long-term consequences of revealing personal details online. He said, "There's this youthful bravado, 'Nothing bad can happen to me.'"[2] Young adults also are not often thinking as far ahead as college and a career, so they may not be choosing what to post online with the idea that someone other than their friends will eventually see it.

In other cases, privacy may be violated without the user even knowing it. Once a picture or post goes online, users are powerless to stop others from sharing their content to other sites. In addition, some applications, or apps, to enhance social network profiles require users to share personal information with the app developer. Once that information is in the developer's hands, the user has once again lost control and privacy.

The supporters of online social networks believe that despite the risks, social networking can be good for society. "We need to keep in mind that the benefits of this interactive technology far outweigh the risks," said Robert Leri, a school district technology and information director. "When it's used in a positive way, it can be an extraordinary tool."[3]

CHAPTER 1

The History of Social Networking

Broadly defined, social networking describes using a website (also called a site) or other type of online communication that allows people to interact with each other. Social networking takes many forms: blogs, message boards, instant messenger apps, and social media websites such as Twitter, Facebook, and Google+. These sites have changed over the years as technology has advanced, and the ones that have not adapted have fallen out of use or gone defunct. People's experiences with social networking, however, are as different as the choices they make online.

The Invention of the Internet

The Internet and the World Wide Web are so deeply ingrained in people's lives today that it is hard to imagine a time when they did not exist. Although the terms are often used interchangeably, they actually refer to two different things. The Internet evolved through the efforts of several government agencies and university scientists. To ease communications between computers at universities and research centers, they devised a way for computers on the different networks to "talk." This system of communication eventually became the Internet. As the Internet grew, it connected millions of computers around the globe and formed a communication network. The development of the Internet laid the infrastructure for social networking.

Early Internet applications allowed people to communicate in small groups through closed networks. As the Internet grew and became an open network, the number of people using the network increased. They could connect more freely and publicly than ever before.

Early Internet use was not as simple as it is today. Telephone lines and modems connected computers physically to the Internet. This was called dial-up Internet, and when the Internet was being used, the telephone line could not be. Actually getting the information out of the Internet was also not simple. Websites did not exist. Data sharing was not user-friendly. Without a technical background, information was difficult to find.

The Creation of the World Wide Web

Using the Internet became easier in 1991 with the launch of the World Wide Web. The web was a new system designed to create, organize, and link documents and web pages so that people could easily read them over the Internet. While the Internet was the system of networks to connect people, the World Wide Web provided the means for people to use that connectivity.

British computer scientist Tim Berners-Lee designed the World Wide Web. He created the HTML coding system for web pages and the addressing system that gave each web page a specific location, or URL. The World Wide Web brought the Internet to life.

The next step in creating an easy-to-use Internet was the development of the web browser. Browser software communicated with the Internet. The software translated web pages and data into an easy-to-read format on computer screens. Browsers such as Netscape and Internet Explorer were the first of their kind; they helped people of all ages and backgrounds use the Internet. Today, browsers include Google Chrome, Firefox, Safari, and others. The creation of the World Wide Web and web browsers enabled the Internet to grow at a rapid pace. By 2006, 73 percent of American adults were Internet users.

Netscape was one of the very first Internet browsers.

For most of the 1990s, the web was a provider of information. Companies and organizations registered web addresses and created websites to provide information to the public. People used this information passively. They read and absorbed it but did little to add to or change what they found online.

People Influence the Web

Around 2002, the way in which people used the Internet and World Wide Web began to change. A trend emerged of users creating and uploading their own content onto the web. The term "web 2.0" surfaced to describe this second level of use for the World Wide Web.

Although the underlying technology of the web had not changed, the change in how people used it made the web more interactive. People could post writing, pictures, video, and music on the web and invite others to view and comment on them. They were no longer just absorbing the information in front of them. Now, they were creating and adding to it. This dramatic change in the Internet's use opened up a whole new world of possibilities. People were eager to join in and explore.

Social Networking vs. Social Media Platforms

There is some disagreement in the online world about whether sites such as YouTube, Twitch, Twitter, and Instagram are social networking websites or social media platforms. The difference between the two is that networking websites create connections between people who interact with each other, while media platforms mainly allow people to see what others are saying. For instance, some people argue that Twitter is a social media platform because it is often used for one-way communication, especially by companies and celebrities. According to Will Oremus, the senior technology writer for *Slate* magazine, "Twitter's most influential users do not tweet with the expectation that they'll be heard only with the people who follow them directly. Rather, they treat the platform like

In the interactive web 2.0 environment, online social networking took hold. Social networking was fluid. Its form was constantly changing and being updated. Through it all, the primary goal of online networking users was to socialize with other people. The form people chose to use was simply a tool to help them achieve their goal.

The Rise of Blogging

Some of the earliest social networking occurred on blogs. A blog—short for the term "web log" ("log" is another word for journal)—is a web page that functions as an online journal or diary. Blog websites created tools that let users easily post entries and photos on a personal web page. The blogger did not need specific technical knowledge to post content on the web page. Instead, most blog tools made posting as simple as using a basic word-processing program. Suddenly, almost anyone could post content to his or her own web page.

Early bloggers posted diary entries for other users to read. As social networking evolved, the blog websites added features to make the experience more interactive. Readers now had the

it's a one-way TV interview, using Twitter to break news, to win arguments, to build their brands, to hone their public personas."[1] In the same vein, people have become famous through YouTube, and for some of these vloggers–video bloggers–making videos is a full-time job that earns them millions of dollars. Many people watch videos without ever commenting or subscribing to channels. This has led some to say that it is a media platform rather than a networking site.

Some people disagree with the idea that websites such as these cannot be considered social networking. It is still possible for people to mention others in their tweets, comment on YouTube and Twitch videos, and make connections on Instagram. It seems that social websites are evolving to become part social networking and part social media platform.

1. Will Oremus, "Twitter Is Not Dying," *Slate*, May 1, 2014. www.slate.com/articles/technology/technology/2014/05/twitter_is_not_dying_it_s_on_the_cusp_of_getting_much_bigger.html.

ability to respond to blog entries by posting comments to the blogger. The blogger, in turn, could reply to the post in another comment or diary entry.

LiveJournal was one of the first blogging websites. Founder Brad Fitzpatrick created the site in 1999. He originally designed it as a tool to keep in touch with friends. Prior to blogging websites such as LiveJournal, bloggers needed a lot of technical skill and patience to post blogs. The introduction of LiveJournal made blogging much simpler for the average user. LiveJournal also carried a strong social element to its blog by allowing users to build a "friends list." Through this, users could check in on their friends' latest journal posts. The site became incredibly popular for several years, but after a series of bad marketing decisions—most notably, deleting hundreds of users' journals without warning in 2007—many of its users turned to other blogging websites.

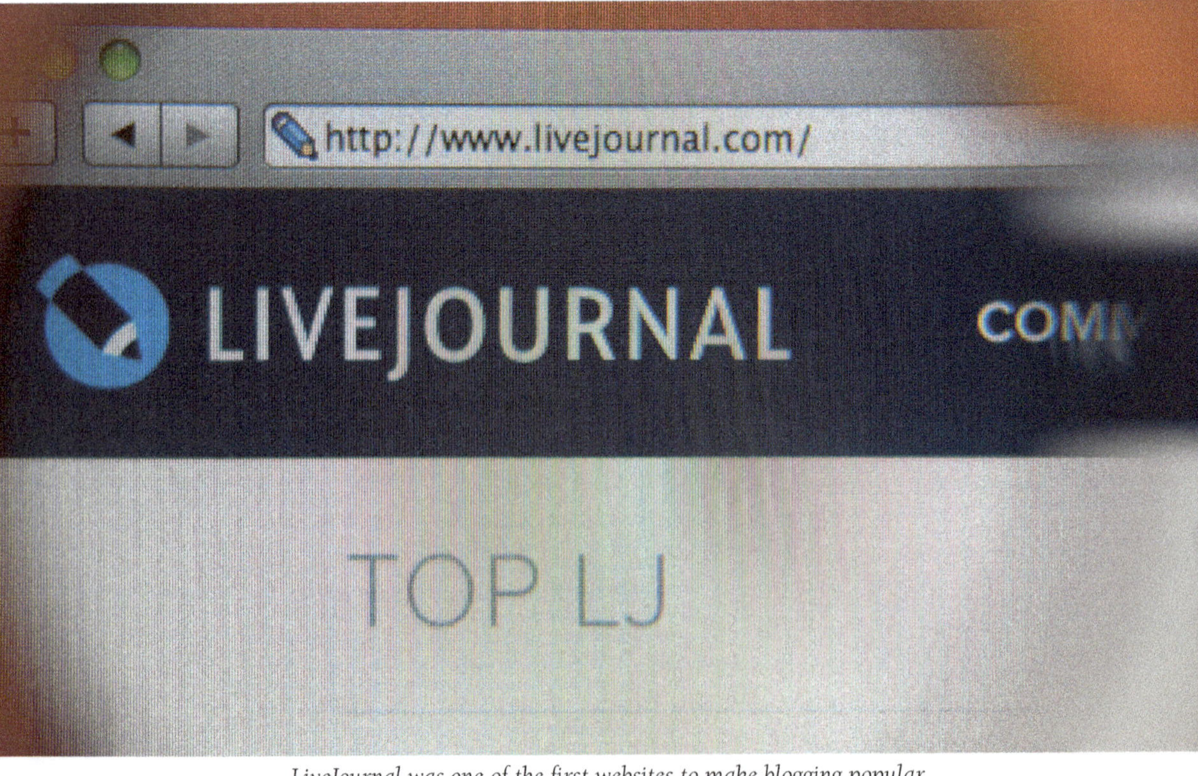

LiveJournal was one of the first websites to make blogging popular.

Social Media Gains Popularity

At the same time that blogging's appeal was growing, some social networking websites appeared. These websites encouraged online social connections. Early websites such as SixDegrees—the very first social media website ever created—and Friendster allowed people to manage a list of friends. One drawback to these websites was that they did not offer users the ability to publish content such as blogs.

Social networking websites often begin with a group of founders sending out messages to friends to join the network. In turn, the friends send out messages to their friends, and the network grows. When members join the network, they create a profile. Depending on the website, users can customize their profile to reflect their interests. They also begin to have contact with friends, acquaintances, and strangers.

A DESIRE TO CONNECT

"When you give people a new way to connect with other people, they will punch through any technical barrier, they will learn new languages–people are wired to want to connect with other people." –Marc Andreessen, software engineer and cofounder of Netscape Communications Corporation

Quoted in Thomas L. Friedman, *The World Is Flat: A Brief History of the Twenty-first Century*. New York, NY: Farrar, Straus & Giroux, 2006, p. 68.

Founded in 2002, Friendster used the model of friends inviting friends to join in order to grow its network. It quickly signed on millions of users. Unfortunately, as the website grew larger, technical issues surfaced. Painfully slow servers made it difficult for users to move around the site. Additionally, management enforced strict policies on fake profiles. These false profiles, or "fakesters," as they were known, were deleted by the site. This approach turned off users. Eventually, Friendster began to lose members in the United States.

Fellow networking website SixDegrees shut down in 2000. Within a few years, these early social networking websites found their popularity declining. At the same time, a new social networking website called MySpace was beginning to take off.

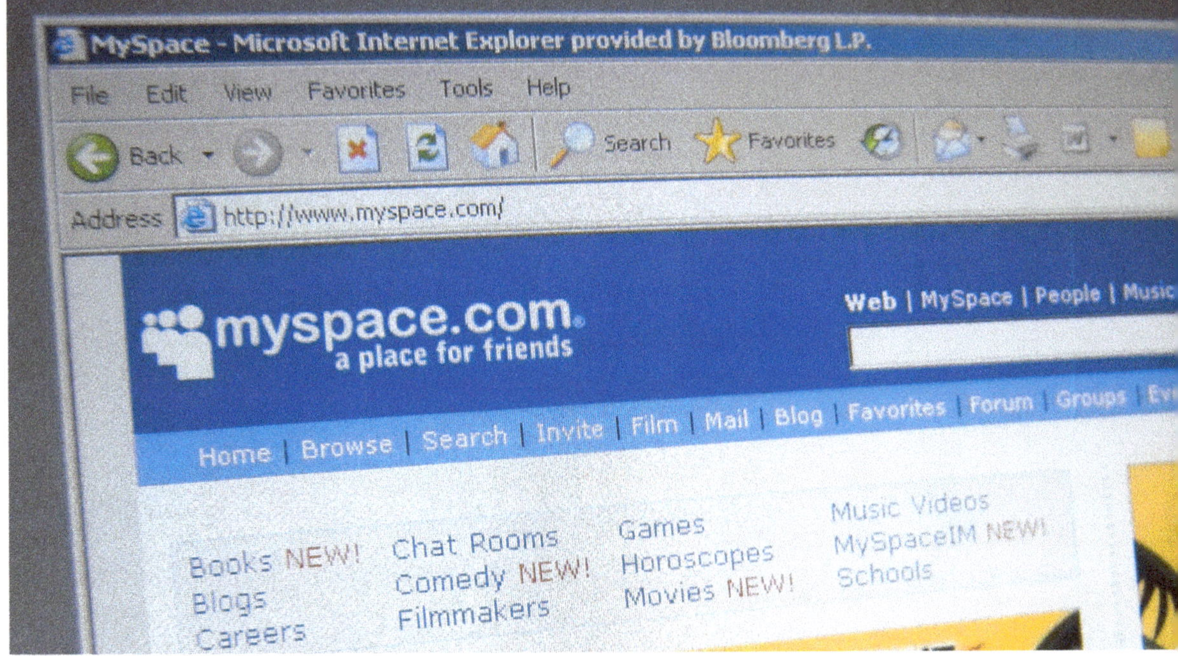

MySpace was popular in the early 2000s because it was the only website that let people connect with friends and personalize their own profiles with pictures, music, and a blog.

MySpace brought together the social features of networking websites and the publishing capabilities of blogs. The combination of the two tools struck a home run with teens. Young people were looking for a more social way to blog. MySpace provided the solution.

In 2003, Tom Anderson and Chris DeWolfe launched MySpace in Santa Monica, California. As music fans, the pair designed the site as a place to promote local music acts. They also wanted to be able to connect with other fans and friends.

On MySpace, users created a website with a personal profile. Then, they invited other users to become their friends. According to DeWolfe, the bands were a great marketing tool in the beginning. He said, "All these creative people became ambassadors for MySpace by using us as their de facto promotional platform … People like to talk about music, so the bands set up a natural environment to communicate."[4]

SO CLOSE, YET SO FAR

"With social networks, there's a fascination with intimacy because it simulates face-to-face communication. But there's also this fundamental distance. That distance makes it safe for people to connect through weak ties where they can have the appearance of a connection because it's safe." –Michael Wesch, associate professor of cultural anthropology at Kansas State University

Quoted in Alex Wright, "Friending, Ancient or Otherwise," *New York Times*, December 2, 2007. www.nytimes.com/2007/12/02/weekinreview/02wright.html.

Anderson and DeWolfe were determined to keep MySpace an open website. Anyone could join the community, browse profiles, and post whatever they wanted. User control was one of their founding principles. It also made initial financing hard to find. According to Anderson, "We'd get calls from investor types who wanted to meet us. They would say, 'Your site isn't professional. Why do you let users control the pages? They're so ugly!'"[5]

In the meantime, MySpace continued to sign people up. Teens and young adults loved the website. They flocked to create their own profiles. The ability to customize pages, load music, and share videos added to the MySpace appeal.

Unlike other early social networking websites, MySpace gave users a media-rich experience. Users could express themselves on their profile by adding music and video clips. At the same time, they could socialize with friends. MySpace made social contact easier with tools such as e-mail, comment posts, chat rooms, buddy lists, discussion boards, and instant messaging.

MySpace brought together the ability to express oneself and to socialize in one place.

The timing was perfect. Over the next two years, MySpace grew at a tremendous pace. The website's success brought attention from investors. Rupert Murdoch, famous for his media empire, wanted to buy MySpace. Murdoch had interests in television, film, newspapers, publishing, and the Internet. In 2005, Murdoch purchased MySpace for $580 million.

By early 2008, MySpace had grown to a mind-blowing 110 million active users. It signed up an average of 30,000 people every day. One in four Americans was on MySpace. The website had become the giant among social networking websites. It was the most trafficked website on the Internet.

MySpace's influence reached outside of the United States. The company built a local presence in more than 20 countries, including the United Kingdom, Japan, Australia, and Latin America. In a few short years, it had become a worldwide cultural phenomenon.

Facebook: A Social Media Giant

The success of MySpace in the social networking arena spurred the development and redesign of many other online social networks. Some websites appealed to a general audience. Others developed to serve specialized communities, such as LinkedIn for job-seekers and MyChurch for Christians.

Facebook was one website that emerged as an alternative to MySpace. In February 2004, Harvard student Mark Zuckerberg launched Facebook. The website began as a closed network for college students. Closed networks only allow users to join if they meet certain criteria. In contrast, websites such as MySpace and Friendster were open social networking websites. Anyone could sign up for an account.

As a closed college network, Facebook grew by adding more colleges to its network. By the end of 2004, Facebook had almost 1 million active users. As Facebook's popularity grew, it expanded beyond colleges to high school and international school users. At this point, however, the website was still restricted to a limited pool of student users.

In 2006, Facebook made a pivotal decision. It opened the network to the general public, expanding beyond its original student base. As of 2017, it is one of the three most visited websites on the Internet, along with Google and YouTube.

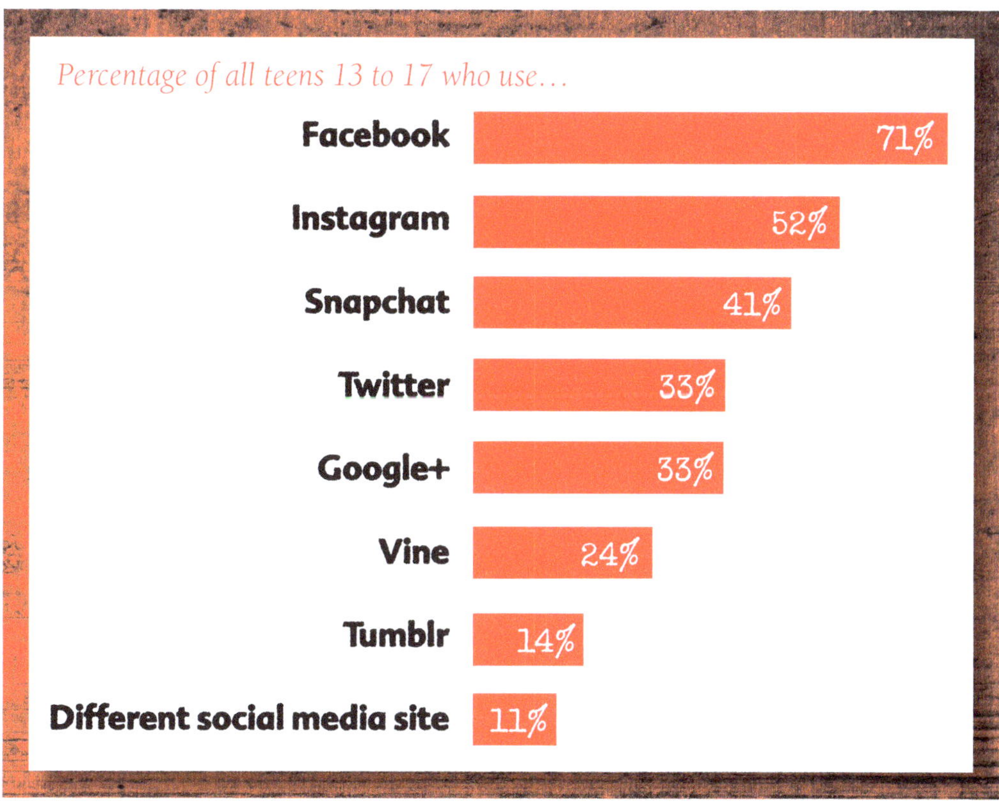

This data from the Pew Research Center shows that Facebook is the social networking website with the most member profiles among teens.

Open and closed social networks have advantages and disadvantages. Open networks allow people to make more connections; for instance, a person from New York and a person from Singapore can become Facebook friends. This would not be possible if the website were only open to American college students. On the other hand, open access means that users can receive messages or friend requests from anyone. Fortunately, Facebook users can choose to block anyone they do not wish to be in contact with. Most other social media websites have this feature as well.

Closed networks are generally smaller. As such, there is a greater chance a user will know other members both online and offline. However, being closed also limits a social network's ability to grow and attract new users.

While MySpace has stayed mostly the same over the years, Facebook has constantly changed and adapted. When Facebook let people develop games and apps for the site in 2007, it dethroned MySpace as the most popular social networking site.

The Future of Social Networking

Online social networking evolved into a full multimedia experience with the arrival of video- and photo-sharing websites. Users can upload visual content to share with friends and other users.

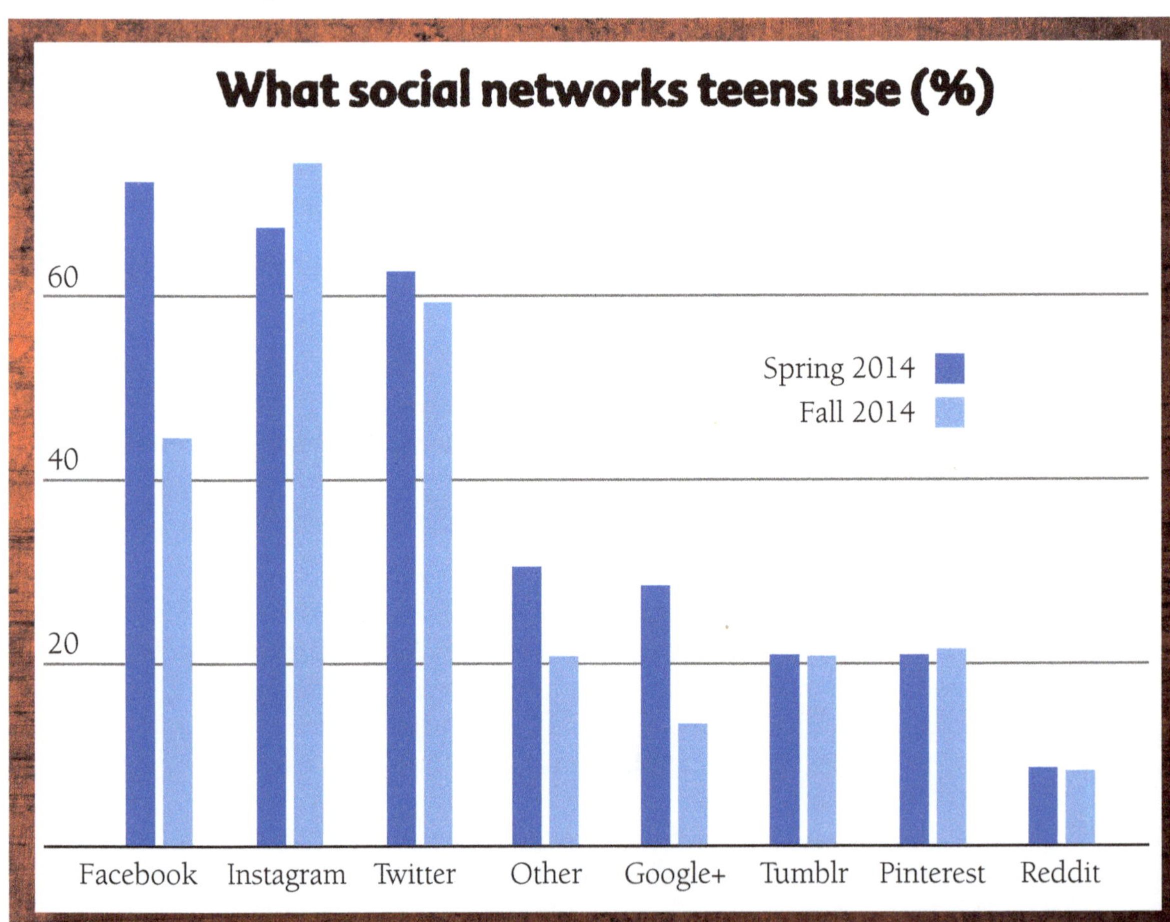

Teens' use of Facebook has been declining dramatically, as this information from the Washington Post *shows.*

Early photo-sharing websites such as Flickr enabled users to transfer digital photos online to share with others. Users decided whether to share their photos publicly or limit access to private groups. People could also use the website's features to organize and store pictures and video. Later, Instagram became more popular because this site made it easier to connect with friends,

Becoming a Savvy Surfer

Today, it is easier than ever before for people to make their own websites, blogs, and YouTube videos. The Internet is not monitored by anyone, which means a lot of the information out there is inaccurate. For instance, someone with no knowledge of personal finance could write a blog about how to make a lot of money in the stock market. Increasingly, the responsibility of evaluating the accuracy of web information falls on the user's shoulders. The following are useful items to look for when evaluating information on the web:

- *Who is the author and what are his or her credentials?*
- *Is the information from a known and respected source?*
- *Can you contact the author?*
- *Can you confirm the information with another source? Is the information documented with cited sources?*
- *Is the information current?*
- *If there are links on the site, do they work? Do they link to reputable sources?*
- *What level of accuracy is needed?*
- *Is the site fair and objective? Or is it biased toward one side of an issue?*
- *Is the site designed for information or for recreational purposes?*
- *Does the Web site creator benefit in some way from the information presented?*[1]

1. Frances Jacobson Harris, "Elements of Web Site Evaluation," University Laboratory High School Library, November 2007. www.uni.uiuc.edu/library/computerlit/evaluation.php.

search for specific photos, and change the way pictures look through the use of filters. Snapchat also became a very popular app and a strong competitor of Instagram.

The most popular video-sharing website is YouTube. Since its beginning in 2005, when people would mostly post personal videos to share with their friends, it has turned into a hugely popular website. Vine is another video-sharing site that has become common in recent years, although nowhere near as popular as YouTube.

Social media websites will keep evolving in the future. Old ones will fade and new ones will take their place. Sites such as Tumblr, Pinterest, Reddit, and Google+ are visited every day by millions of people, but no one knows how long their popularity will last. Even now, some say that Facebook is on the decline. It used to be reserved only for young adults; now people of all ages have profiles, and some teens are beginning to either leave Facebook or not sign up at all. The Pew Research Center reports that Facebook is still used by 71 percent of people between the ages of 13 and 17, although most have more than one social media account, and many have profiles they never use. Twelve-year-old Alek said he created an account so he could play a game that required logging in through Facebook, but he never uses the website to connect with friends. Instead, he prefers Instagram: "I actually use it, my friends are on it, and Instagram is a lot more interesting than Facebook ... You can do a lot more things [with Instagram]."[6]

People Are Social Creatures

The popularity of online social networking has prompted researchers to explore the similarities between online social networks and tribal societies. Irwin Chen, an assistant professor at Parsons School of Design, said, "Orality [talking] is participatory, interactive, communal and focused on the present. The Web is all of these things."[7] In other words, even though people are typing what they put online, it feels more like talking than writing because they often get immediate responses.

Michael Wesch teaches cultural anthropology at Kansas State University. He studied how people form social relationships while living with a tribe in Papua New Guinea. He compared the tribe to online social networking. "In tribal cultures, your identity is completely wrapped up in the question of how people know you," he said. "When you look at Facebook, you can see the same pattern at work: people projecting their identities by demonstrating their relationships to each other. You define yourself in terms of who your friends are."[8]

Despite the connections between social networks and tribal cultures, significant differences exist. In tribal societies, relationships form through face-to-face contact. Social networks allow users to hide behind a computer screen. Tribal societies embrace formal rituals. Social networks value a casual approach to relationships.

Millions of people across the world have joined online social networks. Perhaps their popularity stems from people's natural desire to be part of a community. According to Lance Strate, professor of communication and media studies at Fordham University, social networking "fulfills our need to be recognized as human beings, and as members of a community. We all want to be told: You exist."[9]

CHAPTER 2

How Social Networking Changed Everyday Life

Social networking has become so much a part of the average American's daily life that it is now harder to find someone who does not have an account than someone who does. The widespread use of smartphones is one reason why so many people go online so often. According to a 2015 Pew Research Center report entitled "Teens, Social Media and Technology Overview," 92 percent of teens go online every day, and only 1 percent of those do not use a mobile device to do so. As many as 76 percent have created a profile on a social networking website, and 71 percent reported having profiles on more than one website.

The type of social networking young adults use varies depending on factors such as age and gender. People between the ages of 15 and 17 are more likely to use Facebook, while people ages 13 and 14 are more likely to use other websites or apps instead. Girls are more likely than boys to use most social networking websites, and they make up most of the user population of some of those sites. For example, 61 percent of girls use Instagram, compared to 44 percent of boys; however, the gap between the sexes is much smaller for Twitter, where 37 percent of users are girls, and 33 percent are boys.

Other factors that influence who is using which social media sites include race, income, and location. For instance, anonymous sharing sites such as Whisper or Yik Yak are most popular with Hispanics, while Twitter and Instagram are most popular with African Americans. Overall, the study highlighted that it is impossible to say that one particular social media network is popular with all young adults.

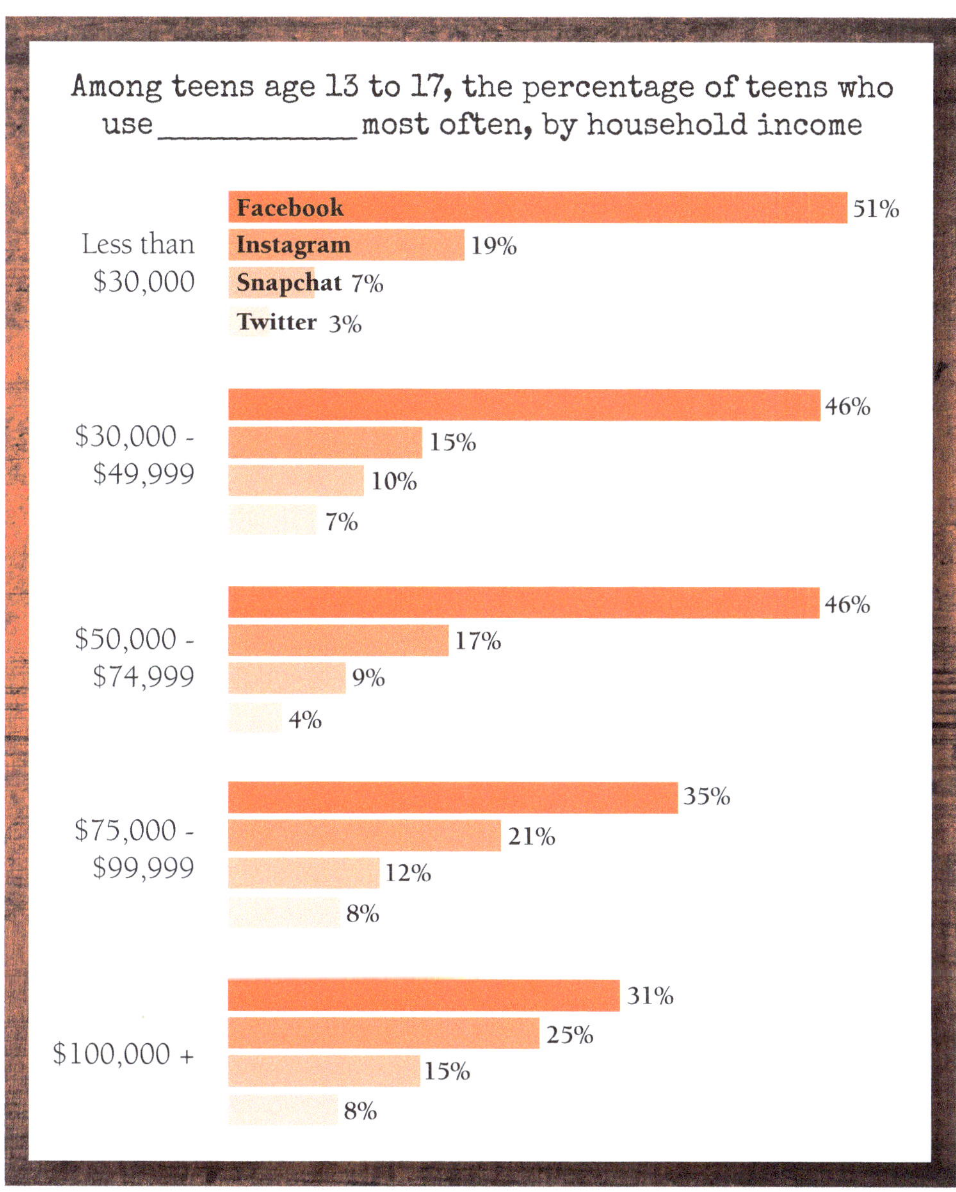

Income is one of many factors that influence who uses which social media website, as this data from the Pew Research Center shows.

Using the Internet to Connect

Many people have commented on the way technology has changed people's lives in the last three decades. Some say that young people today are addicted to their phones, giving up in-person social interaction to see what might be happening online. One study found that "54 percent [of millennials] said they experience a fear of missing out if not checking social networks."[10] However, others argue that being social online is not any less valid than being social in person. They also say that before phones and computers, people used other things that distracted them from having in-person conversations. Keith N. Hampton, a professor in the Department of Media and Information at Michigan State University, said,

> *Consider "what a strange practice it is … that a man should sit down to his breakfast table and, instead of conversing with his wife, and children, hold before his face a sort of screen on which is inscribed a world-wide gossip." These words ring as true today as when they were written, in 1909. They were … [observations] about how morning delivery of the newspaper was undermining the American family.*[11]

People typically believe that young adults use their computers and phones to avoid interaction, but in fact, the opposite is often true. For many teens, technology increases their social connectedness. Online message boards such as Reddit allow teens to share their thoughts with friends and strangers, the same way they might if they participated in an offline discussion group. When they are physically hanging out, they may use their phones to watch YouTube videos together, look at photos of a friend's vacation on Facebook, or read each other funny tweets.

THINGS DO NOT CHANGE MUCH

"What you see is all the behaviors you should recognize from your own teenage years. The difference is that now it's less physical and more word based." –danah boyd, principal researcher at Microsoft Research and founder of Data & Society

Quoted in Michelle Andrews, "Decoding MySpace," *U.S. News & World Report*, September 10, 2006. www.usnews.com/usnews/news/articles/060910///18myspace_print.htm.

When they go home, they use the Internet to continue talking to each other through Facebook Messenger, Google Hangouts, or Skype.

The Internet has become a place to connect with friends after school. On the Internet, teens can interact away from parents, even when their parents are in the same room as them and their friends. David Huffaker, a quantitative user experience researcher at Google, wrote in an academic paper that "these activities are important for identity exploration, which is one of the principal tasks of adolescence."[12]

Always in Touch

Long gone are the days of waiting to use the telephone. Teens chat using instant messaging for hours. They check each other's profiles to post comments and keep current on the latest

In the past, people sometimes had to wait hours or days for a response to a letter or phone call. Today, most communication is instantaneous.

happenings. They share details of their lives, talk about concerns, and even get help with school. Online social networks such as Facebook and Tumblr give teens a variety of ways to connect with friends. These networks also enable them to reach many more people in less time.

Cliques and groups form online just like they do in other settings. Most teens choose to communicate with peers within their own social circle. This practice existed well before the introduction of online social networking. It is similar to the unwritten seating chart in the school cafeteria, where the athletes sit in one section and the drama kids gather in another. Online networks are the larger social scene in which teens find their own groups. Teens' experiences with social networks are in large part determined by the company they keep online, who their friends are, and who they allow into their group.

The term "friends" takes on a new meaning in online social networks. Most people create a Facebook, Tumblr, Instagram, or other social media account so they can keep in touch with the friends they already have. However, it is now common for people to send a Facebook friend request to someone they have only met once or twice. These people may gradually become close friends mostly through online interactions. They learn about each other's personality by commenting on statuses and blog posts, liking photos, and sharing videos.

Planning Made Easy

Teenagers thrive on going out and doing things with friends. Social networks such as Facebook have taken planning online. Teens can announce events such as parties, school functions, and even small get-togethers online. Facebook tools help teens send invitations to their friend list, receive RSVPs, and keep an online guest list. Even details such as directions can be posted or linked online.

Beyond private parties, teens use social networks to search for events in their towns that are of interest to them. Facebook displays public events on the Events page under different categories. Teens can browse the postings and decide which ones they want to put on their calendar.

Sharing Thoughts and Feelings

The teenage years are a time of discovery. Teens learn about themselves, their interests, and their talents. Self-expression gives teens an outlet to find who they are and where they want to go in life. Author Brenda Ueland wrote in 1938, "Everybody is talented because everybody who is human has something to express. Try not expressing anything for twenty-four hours and see what happens. You will nearly burst."[13]

Online social networking gives teens new tools to express themselves. Teen writers create poetry, stories, and other kinds of writing on blogs. Artists post drawings and paintings, many of which are at least partially made on the computer. Photographers display their work. Actors and musicians upload videos of skits and performances for others to view.

An important piece of self-expression is feedback from others. People want to know that others are paying attention to them, and social networking websites provide instant feedback. Users can rate or comment on writing, artwork, or music. Positive feedback encourages teens to develop their unique talents and abilities. Online, teens can find support and

People who create art or music can share what they make online and get feedback from other artists.

encouragement, as well as connections with communities of other people who share their skills.

Social networking websites such as DeviantArt and Behance allow people to share their creations with others. However, people also post their artwork to their personal accounts on sites such as Facebook and Instagram. Sharing pictures and video content is widely popular with teens. Most teens report they frequently receive comments on their photo and video content, often sparking an online conversation.

Susannah Stern, a professor at the University of San Diego, researches adolescents' Internet use. She has found that teens have created a rich online world. "It's just marvelous—just very creative, artistic, opinioned, thoughtful," she says. "They're clearly putting a lot of time into their Internet expression, whether it's in the form of a blog or a homepage or instant message or away message."[14]

Developing Independent Thoughts

The teen years are the time when most people start searching for their own identity, rather than simply listening to what the adults in their lives tell them. As teens express themselves online, they also search for their identity and test their growing independence. They search beyond the inner circle of family and friends to explore and develop personal tastes. Online, teens can explore forums and communities. They can visit discussion boards and participate in conversations. Learning different points of view helps teens develop their own beliefs.

Online, teens can find others who share specific interests such as robotics or the environment. Group members share knowledge with each other. Physical location is no longer a barrier. The group may have members from across the country or around the world. Social networks give teens the chance to mingle with peers from different backgrounds and cultures while they develop interests. According to the Pew Research Center, "57 [percent] of teens ages 13 to 17 have made a new friend online, with 29 [percent] of teens indicating that they have made more than five new friends in online venues."[15] Due to factors such as the ages of the new friends, where they

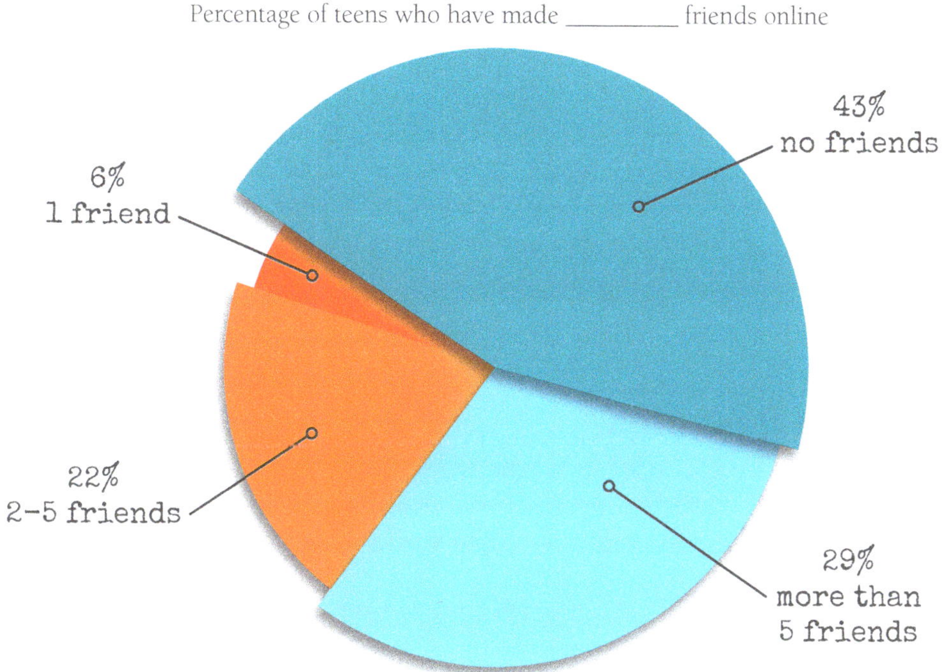

Social media is designed to make meeting new people easy, as this data from the Pew Research Center shows.

live, and the risk that they may not be who they claim to be, most people never meet these friends in person.

Although forums and chat rooms provide an opportunity to meet a wider group of people, there are risks involved. In public forums, there are no restrictions on who can enter and post. People are free to say whatever they want in whatever language they choose. Profanity is common in these spaces. Unfortunately, adults with less-than-honorable intentions can sometimes be found lurking in these spaces. It is important for young adults to remember that personal information—including their real name, phone number, or address—should never be shared on a public site.

WEBSITES CAN ENCOURAGE EDUCATION

"Students are developing a positive attitude towards using technology systems, editing and customizing content and thinking about online design and layout. They're also sharing creative original work like poetry and film ... The Web sites offer tremendous educational potential."
–Christine Greenhow, a learning technologies researcher at the University of Minnesota

Quoted in University of Minnesota, "First-of-Its-Kind Study at the University of Minnesota Uncovers the Educational Benefits of Social Networking Sites," June 19, 2008. www1.umn.edu/umnnews/news_details.php?release=080619_3591&page=UMNN.

Online Obsession

Millions of teens use social networking in a positive way. Unfortunately, with the rise of social networks, negative behaviors associated with the online world have also increased.

Technology has affected society's view of social engagement. Friends sitting together reading books is viewed very differently than friends engaging with their smartphones together.

One major concern parents have expressed is the possibility of young adults becoming addicted to the Internet.

With the Internet constantly at their fingertips, young adults can spend hours online. Sometimes they do not even realize time is passing.

Choosing to Abandon Social Media

Sociologist danah boyd spent several years interviewing young adults of all ages, sexes, races, and economic backgrounds across the United States about how they felt about social media. Andrew, a white high school senior in Nashville, Tennessee, told boyd that he deleted his Facebook after he began to feel as if it were controlling his life. He described the impact this had on his daily life:

> *He said that not having an account cramped his social life. He had more trouble finding out about social activities, and he found negotiating interpersonal relationships more challenging. He explained not being able to look up or "stalk" new friends as one example. To justify his decision, he thought about how older generations managed to get by without Facebook and decided that he was both willing to make and capable of making the sacrifice. "I just kind of remind myself that it's a social networking site," he said, "Which is kind of a smart and dumb idea at the same time to me." Then he added, "Not really. It's a smart idea, but … I should be more mature and get off Facebook." Thinking of his relationship to Facebook as an addiction allowed him to question what had become normative.*[1]

1. danah boyd, *It's Complicated: The Social Lives of Networked Teens.* New Haven, CT: Yale University Press, 2014, pp. 77-78.

Many people who love to read, draw, or play an instrument say the same thing, but in those cases, it is seen as a positive thing. Society's concern seems to be mainly about the technology involved and the fear that teens are using it as a replacement for interacting with the world beyond their computers and phones.

Teens may begin to panic when they cannot access their sites. One 15-year-old girl talked about her friend's reaction to losing a MySpace profile: "I once was with a friend whose MySpace was deleted by hackers, and by the way she was acting, one could think that her family dog had died. She was utterly distraught and was going on and on about how long it was going to take her to get it back up like that again."[16]

Typically, an obsession with something is considered a problem if it starts to interfere with a person's life or health. According to reSTART, the first Internet addiction rehabilitation center in the United States, the symptoms of online obsession can be both psychological and physical. Psychological signs include:

- *Craving more time on the computer and Internet*
- *Neglecting friends and family*
- *Feeling restless when not engaged in the activity*
- *Computer use interfering with school performance*
- *Being dishonest with others*
- *Withdrawing from other pleasurable activities*[17]

Use of the Internet and social media becomes a problem when it interferes with daily life—for instance, losing sleep to spend more time online.

Teens might want to spend more time at the computer, feeling empty or depressed when away from the keyboard and not interacting with friends and family. Physical symptoms include dry eyes, carpal tunnel syndrome, migraines, backaches, and sleep disturbances.

The cofounder of MySpace, Chris DeWolfe, was not worried about addiction to his website. "I don't think it's a concern at all," he said in 2008. "I think it's more substitutional. People are spending less time watching television, and they're spending more time on MySpace."[18]

Sociologist danah boyd agrees that the fear of social media addiction has been blown out of proportion. She believes that young adults use social media as a way to deal with the stress of too much homework, too little free time, and too little privacy. She said, "They aren't addicted to the computer; they're addicted to interaction, and being around their friends … That's how they make sense of the world."[19] She believes that the solution is for parents to give their children more space and allow them to spend more time alone with their friends.

Is Social Media Oversexualized?

In every era, teenagers have sought the attention of the opposite sex. It is a normal and healthy part of adolescent development. Teens worry about how they look; they compete for attention. The pressure to look good has always been especially strong for girls; seeing sexualized models and actresses in magazines and on TV can make girls feel as though they need to look that way in order to get attention or be popular. The rise of social media has created yet another source of social pressure.

Online, teens flirt through instant messaging and profile pages. They post pictures and receive instant feedback with online ratings. Suggestive photos, taglines, and screen names attract more attention online. The desire for attention and positive feedback leads some people, particularly girls, to post increasingly sexual content. Pictures of girls posing in bikinis, in lingerie, and even topless are not uncommon. According to researcher Nancy Jo Sales, who spoke to more than 200 girls across 10 states about the way social media has affected teen girls' lives,

> *The tweens and teens I spoke to were often very troubled by the ways the culture of social media was exerting influence on their self-images and their relationships, with both friends and potential dating partners. They were often highly aware of the adverse effects of the sexualization on girls—but not always sure what to do about it.*[20]

Boys themselves can be another source of this pressure to look sexy. They may feel that it is acceptable to ask a girl to send them naked pictures of herself or to send her naked pictures of their own bodies. However, it is important for young adults to remember that if someone has not requested a naked picture, sending one is considered sexual harassment, and the person who received the picture can press charges with the police. Police advise people who receive unwanted sexual pictures not to delete the photo so it can be used as evidence.

SOCIAL PRESSURE SHAPES BEHAVIOR

"Do boys, too, feel pressure to present a certain image–maybe that of a player who's talking to lots of girls? What do they think when their friends demand nude pictures from girls or harass them online? Do they ever feel guilty about how they treat girls on social media? What, if anything, might get them to change?"

–Anna North, *New York Times* staff editor

Anna North, "'American Girls,' by Nancy Jo Sales," *New York Times*, March 26, 2016. www.nytimes.com/2016/03/27/books/review/american-girls-by-nancy-jo-sales.html

People who receive requests for naked photos should also remember that once the pictures are sent, they have no control over who sees them. They may end up on the Internet or being passed around at school. Even apps such as Snapchat and Skype are not perfectly safe because it is very easy to take screenshots without the other person's knowledge. Additionally, people under the age of 18 who send naked selfies to someone else can be charged with distributing or having child pornography. No one is obligated to send naked pictures to anyone; "no" is always an acceptable answer, even if the person requesting the pictures is unhappy with that answer.

Bullying Moves Online

Social networking has also given traditional bullies a way to move harassment online. Cyberbullying is defined as "bullying that involves the use of e-mail, instant messaging, text messages and digital images sent via cellular phones, Web pages, Web logs (blogs), chat rooms or discussion groups and other information technologies."[21]

However, it can be difficult to define exactly what bullying is. Some people feel that any negative comments on a photo or status should be considered bullying. Others believe there is a difference between arguments and bullying. Most researchers define bullying as when "someone of differential physical or social power subjects another person to repeated psychological, physical, or social aggression."[22] By this definition, cyberbullying is when a person or group of people repeatedly post

Actors Grey Damon and Vanessa Marano attended the Rally to Delete Digital Drama. The rally was hosted by the ABC Family television network and Seventeen *magazine to bring awareness to the issue of cyberbullying.*

mean, rude, or threatening messages to another person's social media profile or post about that person on their own profiles. The victim is typically unable to fight back effectively; his or her responses may be ignored or mocked. Almost all young adults have, at some point, experienced negative comments online. DoSomething.org, a website that advocates for social change, reports that about 43 percent of young adults have experienced some form of cyberbullying. The majority of these teens did not tell parents or other adults about it.

Bullying can happen through threatening e-mails, nasty instant messages, and repeated text messages. In some cases,

Think Before You Post

Even with privacy settings on social networking sites, some posts may be seen by strangers because some social media sites make it very easy to share posts and photos. A person can write a status that is only meant to be seen by that person's friends, but if one of his or her friends shares that status, it will then be seen by people the original writer does not know, who may then share it to their own profiles. This is how things go viral.

Some people in recent years have found that their mistakes have gone viral and had a severe impact on their lives. For instance, in 2012, a woman took a photo of herself at Arlington Cemetery, a military cemetery in Virginia. In the picture, she was standing in front of a sign that said "Silence and Respect," pretending to be loud and disrespectful. Her friend posted it on Facebook, but her photos on Facebook were public, so people who did not know that the photo was meant to be a joke began to share the picture. It made supporters of the military furious, and the woman received many angry Facebook messages. She lost her job and could not go anywhere for almost a year without being followed by the media. Eventually, she found a new job and was able to rebuild her reputation, but stories such as this are an important reminder that it is often difficult to keep things on the Internet private.

bullies set up websites or profiles to make fun of others, impersonate someone else online to post messages, or forward private messages, photos, and videos to others.

One of the biggest differences between traditional bullying and cyberbullying is the anonymous nature of the Internet. The lack of in-person intereaction has led to even more brutal bullying tactics. Because teens cannot directly see or hear how their comments affect the person they bully, they are more likely to send increasingly nasty messages. One school counselor noted that cyberbullying was "the coward's way of bullying because you don't have to have that one-on-one contact … you can do it without having that physical reaction."[23]

CYBERBULLYING IS NOT HARMLESS

"I don't think many adults understand the extent of harm that can be done. We're not talking about some simple e-mails being sent. There's more to this than just a few lines of type and nasty gossip." –mother of a bullied child

Quoted in Candice M. Kelsey, *Generation MySpace: Helping Your Teen Survive Online Adolescence*. New York, NY: Marlowe, 2007, p. 123.

One 19-year-old girl named Daphne told Sales about her experience with cyberbullying. When she was in eighth grade, the friend of a former friend created a YouTube video to promote what he called the Anti-Daphne Movement:

> *Their goal was to get me to kill myself. It was … a 10-minute video. He showed a picture of me … He said I was ugly and that I should kill myself. He told everyone on Facebook, "I'm a member of this movement. If Daphne has ever done anything to you, post about it."*
>
> *It caught on really fast. I had a lot of people writing really mean messages to me and deleting me as a friend [on Facebook]. I had never done anything to these people. At school they would put gross things in my bag, cottage cheese in my binder … It took three months before I got the courage to tell my dad.*[24]

To a victim, online bullying can seem endless. Once someone posts an ugly comment or blog about another teen, the harassment does not end there. The posts sit on social networks indefinitely. They can be passed around through links and e-mails. As each new person reads the negative comment or photo, the harassment begins again. This cycle can repeat over weeks or even months.

The effects of cyberbullying on teens can be devastating. Their schoolwork may suffer, they may have trouble sleeping, and their self-esteem often suffers. Some teens withdraw into depression. Others turn to suicide to end their torment. After 2 years of being cyberbullied, 15-year-old Jeff Johnston hanged himself in his closet. His mother, Debbie, and her husband began lobbying schools, parents, and politicians to put laws and

Text messages that are threatening or demeaning—designed to make someone feel bad about themselves—are one type of cyberbullying.

policies in place to protect other teens. Debbie Johnston said, "I'm not the first parent to experience this, but my son had a purpose to his life. And I would like everyone to know that."[25]

As Daphne's experience proves, avoiding cyberbullies is not as easy as simply turning off the computer, because bullying that starts online may end up happening in person. When the aggression does stay online, teens can block the bully's e-mails, create a new profile or account, and report the bully's offensive behavior to their Internet service provider. Unfortunately, these steps can be time-consuming and may only be a temporary fix. The bully is still online, posting his or her messages in new places where others can see. Some people believe that schools should address the issue. Schools can hold educational seminars for all students to decrease cyberbullying on campus.

The catch, however, is that the majority of cyberbullying occurs off school property and after school hours. Experts disagree on the role of the school in these instances. How far does their control reach into their students' personal lives before it begins to infringe upon their right to free speech?

As teens embrace social networking, the debate continues over the positive and negative aspects of these sites. The concern over new technology is not new to society. Prior generations believed that reading could hurt young girls and comic books would lead to crime. Understanding technology and what teens are doing online will help adults recognize and reward the creative ways teens use social networks. As authors Larry Magid and Anne Collier said, "We need to understand that the Web, as our teenagers use it, is not just a productivity tool or a more convenient way to find information … It's not a tool as we adults see it. It's an extension of teenagers themselves."[26]

CHAPTER 3

Staying Safe on the Internet

Social media has changed the way people interact with each other in day-to-day life and allowed them to connect with people they would previously never have been able to meet. However, it can also be used as a way for people to connect for illegal reasons. Drug dealers, pornographers, and pedophiles have extended their reach through online social networks, creating potential danger for young adults. Extensive media coverage of teens being lured by strangers has stirred concern among adults. These fears are increased by the fact that many people on the Internet post things anonymously. The practice of pretending to be someone else online is called catfishing, and it is very easy to do. A 40-year-old man could believably pass as a 14-year-old girl by creating fake social media accounts, which makes many people suspicious of strangers online. Some seek to ban certain websites entirely, all in the name of protecting minors. However, it is impossible to ban all websites where two strangers could meet, making this an impractical response. Other experts believe the solution is to teach teens to use social networks responsibly.

In 2013, football star Manti Te'o revealed that he had been catfished; the girlfriend he had met online had been fake all along.

Are Strangers More Dangerous Online?

Parents warn their children not to talk to strangers. They give directions on what to do if a stranger approaches them. Run, scream, get away—all are strategies kids and teens learn at home and school. However, what if that stranger is not standing on the corner or hanging out next to the playground? What if that stranger uses a Reddit or Facebook account to find his or her next victim?

From 2004 to 2007, the series *To Catch a Predator*, which aired on *Dateline NBC*, teamed up with an online justice group called Perverted Justice. Volunteers posed as young teens in chat rooms. Quickly, the online discussions turned sexual. The "girl" eventually indicated she was home alone and interested in meeting the men she was chatting with. When the predators showed up, instead of a 14-year-old girl, they found the show's waiting cameras. *To Catch a Predator* was considered controversial. Some people were glad to see predators being exposed before they could continue to harm teens. Others believed that the series did not address the real issue: teens seeking sex online.

When social networking was first becoming popular, the idea that no one online was who they claimed to be was a common fear. Even today, after social media websites put privacy features in place, many parents' biggest concern is that their child will meet a predator online. However, new research shows that despite the fear of predatory adults snatching unsuspecting teens, the reality is quite different. Vulnerable teens who believe they are in love with the person they met online are most at risk for falling victim to a sexual predator.

Adult predators have honed the art of manipulating teens to gain their trust. They use information posted by the teens themselves to become closer to a potential victim. According to Parry Aftab, an Internet safety expert, "If someone knows you … [extremely well,] it's very easy online to be exactly what it is you're looking for—to be your 'soul mate.'"[27] David Finkelhor, director of the Crimes Against Children Research Center at the University of New Hampshire, found that although one in seven young adults will receive a sexual message online, these are easy for teens to ignore and block. His research indicates it is very rare for someone to spend a lot of time pretending to be someone they are not in order to lure unsuspecting children into a meeting because there are much easier targets out there.

Other experts agree. Janis Wolak, senior researcher at the Crimes Against Children Research Center, reported that "the great majority of cases we have seen involved young teenagers, mostly 13, 14, 15-year-old girls who are targeted by adults on the Internet who are straightforward about being interested in sex."[28] In the study, researchers interviewed 3,000 Internet users between the ages of 10 and 17. According to study data, Internet predators used instant messages, e-mail, and chat rooms to meet victims. Once a potential victim was identified, the predator used these online tools to become close with the victim and establish a relationship. This grooming took place over a period of weeks or even months. According to Wolak, "From the perspective of the victim, these are romances."[29] Eventually, the victim, often believing he or she was in love, agreed to meet the predator in person.

Wolak, Finkelhor, and others want teens and parents to be aware of this so they understand where the real danger is. "If everybody is looking for violent predators lurking in the bushes, kids who are involved in these relationships aren't going to be seeing what is happening to them as a crime,"[30] Wolak said.

Some teens are watchful about strangers online. Caitlyn, a 16-year-old MySpace user, said, "There are a lot of creeps out there, and I know it. I don't let anybody add me to their friends list, and I don't accept messages from anybody I haven't met in person."[31] Unfortunately, other teens are not always so savvy. They may turn down friend requests from strangers but post their address on a profile that strangers can see.

Despite the risks, the study found most teens dealt with online strangers appropriately—blocking or ignoring them, leaving websites, or telling them to stop. According to a Pew Internet & American Life Project survey in 2006, 7 percent of online teens and 11 percent of online girls had been contacted through the Internet by a stranger who made them feel scared or uncomfortable. Teens who engaged in risky behavior, such as friending strangers, talking about sex online with strangers, or being rude online, were more likely to attract predators. Wolak said, "One of the big factors we found is that offenders target kids who are willing to talk to them online. Most kids are not."[32]

Parents often worry that young adults are sharing all their personal information on their social media profiles, but the Pew Research Center found that about half of all young adults have posted fake information to their profiles in order to fool people who do not know them personally. Many also keep their profiles private; however, privacy functions on some social media websites—particularly Facebook—can be confusing or change without warning, and people may suddenly realize that their profile is public when all along they thought it was private. It is a good idea for users to occasionally check their privacy settings and make sure they are not sharing anything they want to keep private.

Social Networking for Social Justice

Although people have fears about the Internet, it can often be used as a force for good. One way social media has had a positive impact on the world is its use in the fight for social justice. This is most commonly seen in situations where newspapers are not covering important issues. By using Facebook and Twitter, people can inform each other about things the media either cannot or will not report about.

One important example is the Dakota Access Pipeline (DAPL), an oil pipeline that was proposed to run through the Standing Rock Indian Reservation. Many Native Americans who live on the reservation protested the DAPL because if the pipeline ever broke, it would pollute their drinking water. The DAPL affected a relatively small group of people, so most news networks never mentioned the protest at first. It became a national movement after people shared pictures and videos of the protest on Facebook. After finding out about it, many people donated money, food, and other materials to help keep the protest going. With more people paying attention, major news networks began covering it, but people still relied on live videos posted to Facebook to show them what was really happening at the camp, including some unethical police tactics. Without the help of social media, the protestors might never have gained the public support they did.

With the help of social media, the DAPL protest gained national attention. In response to the public outrage, President Barack Obama halted construction of the pipeline.

Making Friends Safely

The majority of people online are not predators, and many people report making good friends through websites such as Tumblr, Reddit, and Twitter. Especially for people who live in rural, or country, areas where there is not much to do outside of school, this can be a good way to socialize. Often, this happens when someone participates on a website long enough to discover shared interests with the other members. Two people who have Tumblr accounts may find that they have some things in common, begin replying to each other or messaging regularly, and eventually move on to exchanging e-mail addresses or adding each other on other social media websites. They may eventually meet in person, but often they never do.

For some people, their online friends are people they met once or twice in person but are not able to see often, generally because they live too far apart. For instance, *International Business Times* mentioned "two younger children at summer camp [who were] talking about how they wouldn't see each other for another year. To compensate for this, they decided they would meet up in the same place at the same time on Minecraft every day."[33] Cases such as this are not much different than becoming pen pals and writing each other letters; the only difference is that online, the communication is instant.

Meeting strangers online with the intention of becoming friends has become so popular that some apps and websites have been created specifically for that reason. They are similar to dating websites, but their purpose is friendship, not love.

One of the most popular friend websites is Meetup, where people can join groups that fit their interests. The groups host get-togethers that members can attend to meet new people. Some of the groups are based around a specific interest—for instance, someone who likes to knit might join a group where people spend time together while working on their individual craft projects. Others are more loosely based. A group for young women between the ages of 20 and 30 might create events where members who are interested can get together to attend concerts or sporting events, watch movies, or play board games. The only thing the members of such a group need to have in common is their gender and the decade in which they were born.

Meetup is generally safe because it involves a group of people meeting at a public location rather than two people meeting at a private location. However, users must be 18 or older, and there are only a few alternatives for young adults. One of these is Spotafriend, an app similar to the dating app Tinder. People ages 13 to 17 can create a profile and view friends in their area. If two users indicate that they want to talk to each other, the app lets them start chatting. Some people use Spotafriend for dating, but others are interested only in meeting new friends. In either situation, people who meet through the app should be very careful about what personal information they give out. No one should ever tell a stranger their home address, the school they attend, their personal phone number, their current location, or their passwords for other websites.

Warning Signs

Not everyone on the Internet is plotting harm, but it is still a good idea to be careful when meeting strangers online. Some people are not who they say they are; others may not be lying about their personal details—for example, someone who says they are 14 may actually be 14—but this does not automatically make them trustworthy. It is a good practice to guard personal information until it is clear that the person is not trying to take advantage of the situation. Some red flags, or bad signs, to watch out for when interacting with people online include:

- They have no photos of themselves on Facebook or other social media.
- You have no mutual friends on any social media platform.
- They give conflicting information about themselves—for example, constantly giving a different age or hometown. They may try to make up an excuse or explain themselves by saying they mistyped.
- They ask you not to tell your parents or friends that you are talking to them.
- They ask for personal information, such as your address or phone number, soon after contact is made.
- They want to meet in person shortly after contact is made. They may become upset if you refuse or try to convince you to come.
- They ask to meet you in a private place rather than a public place, such as a restaurant. They may invite you to their house or ask to come to yours.
- If you have been friends for a while and your parents approve your plans to meet in person, they cancel repeatedly.
- They make extreme statements, such as that they have never felt this way about someone before, even if you have only talked for a short time.

- They speak sexually or repeatedly comment on your appearance. They may "compliment" you in ways that make you uncomfortable.
- They ask for sexual or nude photos of you, or any photos you are uncomfortable sharing.
- They tell you that you are mature for your age or say that age does not matter in friendships or relationships.
- They ask you for money, even if they seem to have a legitimate need. For example, they may tell you they need help affording medical care or paying their rent.
- They repeatedly tell you they are trustworthy.
- They ask prying questions about your personal life or share personal information about themselves to make you feel that you have to share, too.
- If you let them know that something they are doing makes you uncomfortable, they tell you that you are too mistrustful or that they were joking and you should not take them so seriously.
- They seem to have information about you that you did not give them or that you do not have listed on any of your social media.
- They tell you that you are the only person they can talk to about their problems because you are the only one who understands them. They may try to make you feel responsible for helping them or make you feel guilty if you attempt to end a conversation.
- They threaten to hurt themselves if you stop talking to them.
- They contact you excessively and get upset if you do not respond.
- They seem to have everything in common with you. This may be a sign that they are reading your profile and simply saying they like the same things.
- They become upset if you refuse to do something they ask you to do. They may get angry and call you names or try to make you feel guilty.

- They make you feel uncomfortable, even if you cannot describe why. You are not required to give strangers a chance to prove themselves.

If an online friend has one or more of these red flags, the best thing to do is stop talking to them, block them on all social media websites, and let an adult know what is going on.

PREDATORS USE SUBTLE TACTICS

"The good news is that the vast majority of America's kids are much smarter and much more aware ... But the bad news is, there are a lot of [predators] out there who are still seeking, overwhelmingly for grooming and seduction. This remains a significant problem."
–Ernie Allen, former president of the National Center for Missing and Exploited Children

Quoted in Janet Kornblum, "The Net Is a Circuit of Safety Concerns," *USA Today*, November 8, 2007. usatoday30.usatoday.com/tech/news/internetprivacy/2007-11-07-online-dangers_N.htm.

Drug Dealing Moves Online

One of the fears about social networking websites is that they will make it easier for young adults to buy and sell drugs. Some people believe that it is much easier for teens to find drugs because all they have to do is search for the name of the drug they want. Other people believe that social networking does not make drugs or dealers more accessible; it simply moves in-person interactions online.

Sarah, a 12-year-old from the Midwest, is an example of how social networking can feed and intensify a drug habit. When Sarah felt as if she did not fit in at school, she turned to MySpace and found a community of outsiders like herself. She experimented with drugs before going online, but her online contacts opened up a larger drug world to her. Online, she met drug dealers and other drug users. Several times, she arranged face-to-face meetings with her online contacts. She drifted further and further away from her family, even disappearing for days at a time. The easy access she found online fed her drug habit until she spiraled out of control. Finally, Sarah entered an intensive drug rehabilitation facility.

Because social networking websites are basically uncensored, they have become useful to teens looking to experiment with drugs. According to 16-year-old Edward, the "technology absolutely allows kids more access to drugs. There's no authority on the Internet, no one watches your every move, nobody is all up in your business." Edward himself used the Internet to order prescription drugs and have them sent to his house. Where did he find the doctors who provided the drugs? "Through friends I met on MySpace."[34]

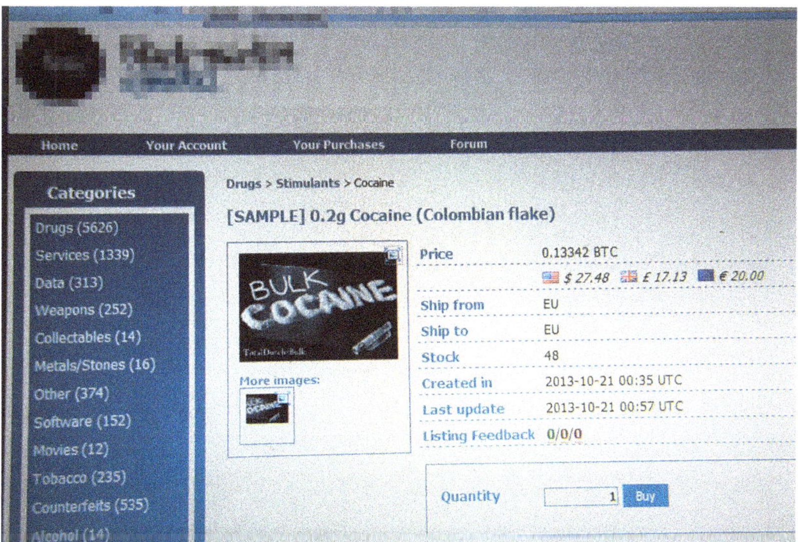

It is not uncommon for people to sell drugs online.

Online, teens can explore drug culture. They can find ways to pass drug tests, post pictures of themselves or others getting high, and get in touch with dealers. Two of the most common types of drugs people sell online are marijuana and prescription drugs. Some teens use their profiles to display their drug activity. Instagram, for example, has seen a growing problem with people posting pictures that show heroin and drug paraphernalia.

Stories such as these and others reported in the media make some people fear that drug culture is out of control online. In May 2016, a Colorado radio station reported that a secret

Facebook group had been created where children as young as 12 were buying and selling drugs illegally. Many people were shocked to find out about the group, and officials recommended that parents monitor and limit their children's social media use. This incident was seen as evidence that social media is making it easier for young adults to find and get drugs.

However, some people disagree with this idea. They point out that the fact that the group was secret means people had to be invited by someone they already knew. The young adults who are likely to go looking for drug groups online are the ones who are already interested in trying them. Buying and selling drugs online also make it much easier to be caught by the police. Although it is clear that it is easy for people to find drugs on social media if they know where to look, it is not as clear whether this is a new problem or simply the continuation of an existing problem.

EVERYTHING HAPPENS ONLINE

"MySpace and the Internet are a reflection of the real world … So if something happens in a town, if it happens in the world, it's likely to happen in cyberspace." –Larry Magid, codirector of Connectsafely.com

Quoted in Laura Marquez, "Teens Find Drugs on Social Networking Sites," ABC News, May 8, 2009. abcnews.go.com/US/story?id=7540003&page=1.

Is Pornography More Readily Available?

In years past, pornography stayed hidden in back rooms and stuffed under beds. Today, pornography has become almost mainstream. Sexual images abound in advertising, television, and films. In fact, some people believe that society has begun to think of porn as a form of sexual expression.

Surrounded by sexual images, it is not surprising that teens on social networking websites are mimicking the behavior they see—posting increasingly sexual photos and talking about sex frequently. Leaked nude photographs and sex tapes of celebrities create a tremendous following when posted online, despite this invasion of the celebrities' privacy. This shows that if a person is the victim of a hacker, photographs they never intended for anyone to see might become public.

Sex scandals catch the public's interest—so much so that some people use them as a way to become famous. In a 2016 scandal, Denver Broncos linebacker Von Miller was blackmailed by a woman named Elizabeth Ruiz. Ruiz threatened to release a sex tape of her and Miller if he did not pay her $2.5 million for the video. When he refused, Ruiz tried to sell the tape to several websites, hoping to become famous the way Kim Kardashian did for her sex tape.

When the media focuses on celebrity sex scandals such as the one involving linebacker Von Miller (shown above), a vicious cycle is created that reinforces the idea that pornography will lead to fame.

The official stance of social networks such as Facebook and Instagram is that pornographic material has no place on their websites; posting explicit photos on these websites will get a user blocked or banned. However, porn is readily available on other websites, and even on Instagram, the website does not always do an adequate job of finding and removing explicit photos. Porn companies make it harder to find their posts by using hashtags that do not describe the photos and videos they post.

This wide availability of pornography has both parents and researchers concerned. Nancy Jo Sales believes that the porn young adults see on social media has created a situation "where boys are taught they have the right to expect everything from social submission to outright sex from their female peers."[35] One 16-year-old girl that she interviewed said, "[Boys are] definitely more forward to us online than in person … Because they're not saying it to our faces."[36] Another girl worried about her

13-year-old cousin: "[S]he posts such inappropriate pictures on Instagram, and boys post sexual comments, and she's like, 'Thank you' … It's child pornography, and everyone's looking at it on their iPhones in the cafeteria."[37]

Who Is Responsible?

Social networking websites can be used for good; they are an excellent way for young adults to connect with their friends and learn more about people outside their community. However, the risks associated with social network use have sparked a conversation about the best way for young adults to stay safe online. Whose responsibility is social network safety? Is it the government's role to intervene and regulate these websites? Should the websites themselves implement stricter guidelines and more effective policing? How should schools and parents educate teens about online safety? What steps should teens themselves take to stay safe? In every situation, there is more than one side to the debate.

Websites Monitor Content

Social networking websites have security teams and procedures designed to sift through activity on their website and flag any illegal or offensive material. Websites monitor user accounts and can remove content, such as nudity, that violates the user agreement. In reality, however, the sheer volume of posts to monitor allows many photos to slip past the safeguard and remain online for teens to view.

While officials acknowledge that dangerous activity does take place on social networking websites, they also stress that these dangers are in every community, online or not. Tom Anderson, cofounder of MySpace, felt that the negative activities happening on his website were nothing new: "Those things happen in any large community … the sense that MySpace is this place where all these bad things are happening is truly overblown."[38]

In 2008, more than 20 high-tech businesses, including Facebook, joined the Internet Safety Technical Task Force. The group's goal is to develop age and identity verification for online users. Facebook also signed agreements with the attorneys general of 49 states and pledged to toughen safety measures online.

In 2012, several news websites reported that Facebook was scanning private chats in order to find people who were taking advantage of the website, especially adults who were targeting teens for sex. Tech website CNET said,

> *Facebook's software focuses on conversations between members who have a loose relationship on the social network. For example, if two users aren't friends, only recently became friends, have no mutual friends, interact with each other very little, have a significant age difference, and/or are located far from each other, the tool pays particular attention.*[39]

Facebook's program works by scanning chats for certain words that have previously appeared in criminals' chats. The company says its employees only look at the chats if the software finds something suspicious. However, evidence has been found that Facebook is also scanning private messages so it can target ads to users more effectively. In 2016, a class action lawsuit—a lawsuit filed by a large group of people—was brought against Facebook for invasion of privacy. Facebook has denied that it is reading people's private messages, but if the company loses the lawsuit, it may be required to stop scanning messages altogether.

Laws Controlling the Internet

Pointing to the threat to children, several government officials and entities have gotten involved in the discussion about social networking safety.

Indiana and Nebraska are two states that have enacted laws against sex offenders. These states' laws prohibit registered sex offenders who are convicted of crimes against children from using social networking websites or programs where people under age 18 are allowed. However, these states have been sued over these laws, as sex offenders say that the number of social networks restricted to people over the age of 18 is so small that the laws effectively prevent them from using the Internet. For example, because Skype is available to people under 18, sex offenders would not be able to use it at all, even if no one on their friends list is a minor. They claim that this means they might have a hard time communicating with friends and family. They also say that the language in some of the laws is too vague, which means it is very easy for them to unknowingly break them.

Most social networks specify that users must be at least 13 to create an account.

At the federal level, Congress introduced the Deleting Online Predators Act in 2006. The act required schools to prevent students from accessing social networking websites and chat rooms unless doing it for an educational reason under the supervision of an adult. It also required public libraries to deny access to social networking websites to children unless they had a parent's consent.

Several groups opposed the act. The American Library Association (ALA) spoke out against the legislation. They claimed that the blanket blocking of websites as directed in the act would block access to some powerful learning applications. The users would no longer be able to take advantage of the full educational opportunities that the Internet offers.

Additionally, boyd warned against blocking teens' access to websites. "Blocking known sites will encourage teens to go further underground and seek out places to socialize that adults are unaware of," she said. "This puts youth at increased risk and means that neither educators nor law enforcement will be around to help."[40]

The act passed in the House of Representatives in 2006 with an overwhelming majority in a 410 to 15 vote, but it stalled in the Senate and was not signed into law.

Schools' Responsibility

Many schools are uncertain where their responsibility falls when students go online. Some worry about the activities and websites that students access while on school property, but what about online activities when students are off campus?

Many schools have decided to deal with the safety issue by simply blocking access to social networking websites from school computers. However, when the students go home, the issue becomes much grayer.

In just one of many incidents, a Chicago school district suspended three middle school students for posting obscene and threatening comments about a teacher on a blog. The school community was divided over the suspension. Some agreed with the school. Others thought the administrators had overstepped their authority. According to Steve Jones, a communications professor at the University of Illinois at Chicago, "It's an open question, because students have been writing these sorts of things for years but have been doing it in their notebooks, where nobody would have ever stumbled across it. With blogs, it's a sign of things to come—we're sort of testing the notions regarding free speech."[41]

Some schools believe they have the authority to punish students who post inappropriate things online, whether they used a school computer or one at home. Others disagree.

Rather than blocking websites entirely, some experts recommend using schools to teach students about online safety. They believe teachers are the best people, aside from parents, to show young people the risks of online behavior and help them deal with risky situations. Educators can show teens how to use these websites in a controlled and supervised environment. Henry Jenkins, director of the Comparative Media Studies Program at MIT, commented, "Historically, we taught children what to do when a stranger telephoned them when their parents are away; surely, we should be helping to teach them how to manage the presentation of their selves in digital spaces."[42]

Parents Need to Be Involved

Given the risks facing teens online, it is not surprising that a number of parents have decided to ban social networking websites entirely from their homes. This approach, however, does not stop curious teens from accessing these websites from a friend's house and creating profiles under a made-up name. Even worse, when these teens do run into problems, they are less likely to report their problems to adults for fear of getting in trouble.

Most experts do recommend that parents stay involved in their child's online life, but opinion is divided on the best way to do this. Some believe that parents should closely monitor what their children do online at all times. Some parents use filtering software to protect teens. These programs block children and teens from accessing inappropriate websites and content. The downside, however, is that these programs also block some useful websites such as search engines. Liz Perle, the former editor-in-chief of Common Sense Media, an organization that aims to improve the media life of kids and families, disagreed with the use of filtering software. "Filters and blocking are absurd for teens," she said. "It's a fool's errand, and you might as well put your kid in a bag. You have to teach kids. They want to explore and see what's out there."[43]

Simple online searches of a teen's name and information can alert parents to any unknown blogs or profiles if they are not using a fake name. Some parents demand their children's social media passwords or install software that keeps track of what their children do online. Keylogging software, for example, keeps track of every word typed on a computer, and it can be installed secretly. Most parents do not go this far, but some may use an app such as GoGoStat or Eye Guardian, which allows parents to view everything their child does on Facebook. These apps require the Facebook user's e-mail and password, so parents cannot monitor their children without their consent. However, some people still feel this is a violation of teens' right to privacy. The apps also do not stop teens from making one Facebook profile for their parents to monitor and another profile for personal use.

The Deep Web and the Dark Web

In today's society, people believe that Google can be used to find anything. It is true that there is a huge amount of information available to people through search engines, but there are also some websites they cannot access. This is known as the deep web. For instance, searching for a specific person's e-mail account will not return results.

The dark web is hidden within the deep web, but it is not the same thing. The dark web is impossible to get to without special software, but once the software has been downloaded, people can access most dark websites the same way they would through Google. This part of the Internet is where many illegal dealings take place. People can buy guns, drugs, fake passports, and other illegal items without leaving an electronic trail for police to trace. Money is not accepted on the dark web; people buy things with electronic credits called bitcoin. Although many people worry about illegal activity taking place on social media websites, the dark web is much more of a threat.

Most parents who monitor their children's social media activity feel that privacy is not a right for minors and that checking up on what their teens are doing online makes them good parents. As a way to protect their privacy even when their parents are watching, many young adults have found ways to code their online messages so their friends understand what they mean, but their parents do not. Some experts, including boyd, believe that parental surveillance does not actually keep teens from doing unapproved things online; instead, they believe it simply forces them to become more creative about hiding what they are doing. The key, many feel, is trust and open communication. If teens feel as though they are able to discuss things with their parents without fear of punishment or judgment, they are more likely to let their parents know what they are doing online.

PARENTS NEED TO BE INVOLVED

"Kids who were experiencing some conflict on social media, be it with a friend or schoolmate, had very elevated levels of distress but that experience was mitigated if their parents were highly involved with monitoring their accounts." –Robert Faris, associate professor, Department of Sociology, University of California Davis

Quoted in Kelly Wallace, "Parents: Here's How to Stop the Worst of Social Media," CNN, October 14, 2015. www.cnn.com/2015/10/04/health/being13-social-media-teens-parents-stress/.

While parents and other groups work to increase the safety of online networks, teens and other users are ultimately responsible for their own actions on these websites. Several simple steps such as limiting profiles to friends only and using password protection features can keep out unwanted attention. Other important steps include keeping personal information private and taking any discussion of sexual and emotional issues off the Internet. Users should also evaluate the benefits and risks of participating in online groups and forums.

Privacy on the Internet

Privacy is an important consideration on social media websites. People want to make sure they give enough identifying information for potential new friends to find them, but not enough to make them vulnerable to strangers. Most people restrict what strangers see on their public profile, but sometimes they overshare to their friends. It is important to remember that anyone is able to take a screenshot of tweets, Facebook posts, Snapchat pictures, or other types of shared content. Once they have those screenshots, they can show them to other people or post them on other websites. Facebook has also been making it increasingly easy for people to share each other's posts through linked websites or texting. Many young adults feel a false sense of security once they make their profiles private, and they often do not think about how the things they post may affect them in the future.

Blogs: Private Journals Made Public

Today's teens have been raised in a digital world. Using online networks to express their thoughts and feelings is a natural extension. Sixteen-year-old Emily turned to the Internet after her mother found her paper diary. "When there were days when I just needed to rant, it felt good. I'd come home after school, and I'd spend, like, an hour typing in everything I did all day … Once I discovered … posting online, it definitely became, 'Why would I write it in a book?'"[44]

Online diaries can be made private, so only the writer or a select group of friends can read them. Tumblr allows users to password protect their blog so that only friends who have the password can read it. Many, however, choose to allow open access, inviting the world to read. Jeremy, a Virginia Tech graduate who signed up for LiveJournal, explained, "Everything everyone's writing online, they want it there because they want it to be read by someone … Having someone read your secret feels better."[45]

Personal Sharing has Increased

According to the 2013 Pew Research Center study "Teens, Social Media, and Privacy," teens post more personal information on their social network profiles than they did in the past:

- *91% post a photo of themselves, up from 79% in 2006.*
- *71% post their school name, up from 49%.*
- *71% post the city or town where they live, up from 61%.*
- *53% post their e-mail address, up from 29%.*
- *20% post their cell phone number, up from 2%.*[1]

The study also found that while the majority (60 percent) of Facebook users make their profiles private, the majority (64 percent) of Twitter users say their accounts are public.

1. Mary Madden et al., "Teens, Social Media, and Privacy," Pew Research Center, May 21, 2013. www.pewinternet.org/2013/05/21/teens-social-media-and-privacy/.

Parents, teachers, and law enforcement officers, however, feel less enthusiastic about posting details of private lives online. Jeremy's mother, Karen, was horrified when she discovered her children kept online diaries. "I just thought it was terrible, horrible. I just couldn't imagine why you would put your feelings and personal comments on something that just went out there."[46]

Most young adults understand that what they are putting on their public blogs can be read and shared by anyone. Some will not write anything they want to keep secret. Others assume no one except their friends will care about what they write, so they will be more open with their posts. Young adults who have blogs do not share the view that they are publishing a private diary; rather, they generally see blogs as a way to keep friends updated about their lives and opinions. Teens who do see blogs as an invasion of privacy are not likely to create one.

Not every blog is an online diary. People create blogs for many reasons: to share recipes, craft ideas, and fashion tips; to give their opinion about politics, books, or television shows; to share funny stories; and much more. Blogging can be done just for fun or as a career.

Different Views on Privacy

How much teens decide to share varies from person to person. The user's age, race, and gender frequently play a role in privacy decisions.

Girls and boys typically share the same kind of personal information, with the exception of cell phone numbers, which boys are much more likely to share than girls. In a 2007 focus group, one high school girl talked about how she decided what to post on her profile:

> *i try to post as little information as possible. there is no way of knowing who is going to see the information posted and i'm really stingy. i don't think it's okay to share last names, date of birth, where i live, anything that will help people identify me. pictures are OK because it's really difficult to find someone if the only thing you know about them is what they look like.*[47]

The 2013 Pew study found that teens ages 14 to 17 are more likely than teens ages 12 to 13 to post personal information on public profiles. Older teens, especially white ones, commonly share photos of themselves and friends on their sites. They are also more likely to disclose their school name, relationship status, and cell phone number.

For teens who do decide to share some or all of their profile with the public, the majority give some false information in the profile. One middle school girl talked about why she posted fake facts: "I don't want anyone to know where I'm from. You don't need the people that you know to be able to read where you're from because they already know."[48] Other teens use fake information for different reasons. One high school boy talked about putting a fake age on his profile: "I say instead of being 14 I'm 15 ... No one wants to talk to a 14-year old. So why not just add another year?"[49]

Users who are careful about keeping profiles and pictures free of personal information may not be so watchful when posting on a friend's profile. A public comment that gives the time and place friends plan to meet allows anyone who sees it to find those people. Someone who shows up uninvited may be annoying at best and risky at worst. Posting about family vacations can also invite trouble. In 2013, *International Business Times* reported that some thieves were using Facebook to find out when people would be away from their homes for a long period of time. When someone posted that they were out of town or checked into another state on Foursquare, they made themselves a target for burglars. Security experts advise not publicly posting about vacations until the trip is over and everyone is back home.

Some teens, however, believe the fuss about online privacy is overblown. Tyler, a high school freshman, thinks that keeping personal information out of social networking defeats its purpose. "I know how annoying it is to look for people and it being impossible to find them," he said. Tyler listed his high school name on his profile so that friends could more easily find him. He does acknowledge that keeping personal information public has its risks. "But I'm not going to be stupid about it," he said. "We all get messages from weird old men who are like 'hi'—but nobody replies to them."[50]

Researchers such as boyd believe that teens who grew up in the Internet era have a different expectation of privacy than adults who did not because young adults have created a social code surrounding the Internet—one that no one talks about, but everyone knows. For instance, many people see no problem with posting where and when they want to meet up because they do not believe anyone would be rude enough to show up uninvited. The same is true for posts that anyone can see. According to boyd, there is a type of etiquette—unwritten social rules that decide what is and is not polite—about these posts similar to the etiquette people follow in person:

> *For example, even when two people happen to be sitting across from each other on the subway, social norms dictate that they should not stare at each other or insert themselves into the other's conversations. Of course, people still do these things, but they also feel a social responsibility to avert their eyes and pretend that they cannot hear the conversation taking place. What's at stake is not whether someone* can *listen in but whether one* should.[51]

Most people understand that just because they can hear a conversation does not necessarily mean they can join it. Many teens argue that posts on the Internet operate the same way.

People who do not follow this online etiquette may get a reputation for being nosy or annoying, just as they might in real life. However, it is important to remember that people who intend to do harm are willing to break social etiquette, so it is still a good idea to be cautious of who can see private information online.

What Are Third Parties?

Even users who restrict access to their profile may be vulnerable to privacy risks. For instance, users share private information every time they use a third-party app or log in to a website with their Facebook username and password. Third-party apps are apps that can be used on social media but are not made by the website. For instance, if people do things such as take a quiz, play a game, or learn their horoscope through Facebook, they are often leaving Facebook and visiting another website. These third parties typically require users to let them see certain things, such as the user's public profile, friends list, and interests. If the user declines, the app or website will not let them take the quiz or play the game. Additionally, Facebook makes certain information—such as a user's name, gender, username, and profile picture—available to anyone, including third parties.

Facebook insists that its application developers must follow strict policies and standards that limit what they can do with user information. However, most security experts agree that access to too much personal information is not a good thing. "I suspect that there's a whole lot of clicking without a lot of thinking," said Mary Madden, a senior researcher at the Pew Research Center's Internet & American Life Project. "So much of this sharing happens in a way that users don't see the consequences. It's kind of a big, black hole."[52]

The 2013 Pew study found that the majority of teen social media users are either unaware or unconcerned about how much of their private information can be given out to third parties. Most people click yes when the apps ask for permission because they do not think there is anything wrong with letting an app see information they have already made public. However, since users cannot tell who made the app, they may unknowingly be opening themselves up to hackers. "You want to be social with

To protect its users, Snapchat is no longer compatible with third-party apps.

your friends, but now you're giving 20 guys you've never met vast amounts of information from your profile," warned Chris Soghoian, a cyber-security researcher and activist. "That should be troubling to people."[53]

Snapchat addressed the problem of third parties in 2014 when an app called Snapsaved was hacked and 90,000 private photos were leaked, which led Snapchat to remind users that third-party apps are often unsafe. A year later, it changed the way Snapchat works so third-party apps are no longer compatible with it.

Some apps and websites use a trick called social engineering, which is when someone fools another person into giving them personal information. Online, it is often known as phishing. There are many different ways someone can be phished. A phisher may create a third-party app that sends them people's information when they log in to the app with Facebook. Someone may receive a pop-up box claiming that another user is trying to impersonate them and to prove their identity, they must enter personal information, such as an e-mail password or birthday. A phisher may send a private message to a Facebook user asking for money or personal information. It is a good idea never to give out personal information over the Internet and not to take quizzes or play games on Facebook if the source of the quiz or game is unknown.

USE COMMON SENSE

"In the beginning, I kind of posted whatever without really thinking about it. I could have saved myself a lot of misery had I just sat down and used my common sense."
–Michael Guinn, college student expelled for content on Facebook profile

Quoted in Janet Kornblum and Mary Beth Marklein, "What You Say Online Could Haunt You," *USA Today*, March 8, 2006. www.usatoday.com/tech/news/internetprivacy/2006-03-08-facebook-myspace_x.htm.

Who Can Find Social Media Users?

As noted in the Pew study, most users are at least thinking about privacy decisions and taking steps to protect themselves from strangers online. However, what happens when the person reading a profile is not a stranger? As the popularity of social networks continues to grow, users find themselves online with more than just a circle of friends. Suddenly, parents, teachers, university admission officers, and future employers are online and reading user profiles.

One of the biggest risks for social network users is posting content without thinking about who exactly will be reading it. What seems like a funny picture to share with friends may not be so impressive to a teacher or college admissions counselor. According to child psychologist David Welsh, "Most of the situations I'm running across in my practice are kids being caught by surprise, sort of, at how incredibly public and accessible [the blogs are] … it's an odd mix of a perceived anonymity with an obviously very public forum."[54] He believes that having usernames instead of real names can lead to a false sense of security.

As more parents ask to friend or follow their teens online, young adults may struggle with separating the content intended for friends from what they want to share with other adults, including their parents. As parents go online, they may not like what they see. In one extreme example, in 2012, a father uploaded a video to YouTube of himself reading a post his daughter wrote. Even though she had made the post private, her father ended up

Teens and their parents often have differing ideas of how much privacy young people should be allowed to have online.

finding it. In the post, she complained that her parents expected her to do too many chores around the house. After reading the post, he made it clear that he thought she was disrespectful, then shot her laptop with a gun. Some people applauded this move as good parenting, while others thought he had crossed a line. Most parents do not go so far as to destroy their children's computers, but they may restrict Internet access.

Some teens design their sites knowing that parents may be watching. One high school girl in the 2007 Pew focus group talked about the fact that she only posted innocent pictures online: "Like if my Mom saw it I wouldn't care. I'm really careful with that whole MySpace thing. I've heard of employers not hiring people because of it. So I just put things up there that if my Grandma or Mom saw it I wouldn't care. It wouldn't be a big deal."[55] A middle school girl agreed, "When I'm on MySpace I will never put anything on it that I wouldn't want my parents to see."[56]

In addition to parents, teachers and schools are getting involved with social networks. Where the school's responsibility lies is a blurry line. Do they have a right to monitor students' online activities after school and off campus, or is too much involvement a violation of students' right to privacy?

Some schools draw the line when social network activity begins to affect the school and other students. In Costa Mesa, California, a middle school expelled a student for posting threats against a classmate. In addition, 20 of his classmates received suspensions for viewing the posts.

"We are trying to figure out how our school rules relate to this type of behavior,"[57] said Meredyth Cole, the assistant head of the Madeira School in the Washington, D.C., area. She decided to send a letter to the parents of her private school students warning them about students' use of social networking sites.

STUDENTS HAVE A RIGHT TO FREE SPEECH

"The best way to counter bad speech is with good speech, not with suspensions and censorship ... School officials should be extremely cautious before attempting to limit student expression on a private Web site maintained off school grounds."
—Sam Chaltain, former codirector of the First Amendment Schools Project

Quoted in Paula Reed Ward, "Schools Perceive Threat to Authority in Student Internet Postings," *Pittsburgh Post-Gazette*, February 5, 2006.

Some people believe schools have no right to dictate what young adults do online when they are at home, and the issue has been brought to court in several cases. Tim Trautman, head of the Barrie School in Silver Spring, Maryland, explained his school's policy: "We try ... to say that the boundaries are on school grounds and within school time, but if there is a case that does tend to spill over and directly impact campus life, all of a sudden space and location, the geography of it, becomes less important."[58]

Colleges Look at Social Media

Even college students feel the impact of their social network activities reaching an unintended audience. A 20-year-old student at Iowa Western Community College wrote an entry on his website that some people in his dorm should be shot. When college officials learned of the entry and other threatening posts, they expelled him and banned him from campus. The student protested that the posts were meaningless and the punishment excessive, but he was not allowed to come back to school.

Other students have been suspended or expelled when colleges discover pictures of them drinking underage or posing with drug paraphernalia. However, are these punishments appropriate? "As more students are suspended and disciplined, we're going to need some clear guidance from the courts," urged David Hudson Jr., an attorney at the First Amendment Center in Nashville. "Right now, it is not clear just how far the authority of school officials extends."[59]

NOT EVERYTHING SHOULD BE SHARED

"Just some of the pictures I ran across [on Facebook]—I couldn't believe it ... You can only think: What if one of the big accounting firms comes across this, or a law firm or law school or graduate school?"
—Cheryl Barnard, associate dean of student affairs at Quinnipiac University in Hamden, Connecticut

Quoted in Janet Kornblum and Mary Beth Marklein, "What You Say Online Could Haunt You," *USA Today*, March 8, 2006. www.usatoday.com/tech/news/internetprivacy/2006-03-08-facebook-myspace_x.htm.

In addition to teachers and school administrators, college admissions offices are getting involved in social networks. At Reed College in Portland, Oregon, Dean of Admissions Paul

Marthers admitted that his department reviews an applicant's social networking profiles. In one case, Reed denied admission to an applicant who bragged of plans to beat Reed's financial aid system and posted hostile messages about some Reed officials. "How could we not factor in the life he was having on LiveJournal?"[60] asked Marthers.

High school students need to be aware of what they are posting. A 2013 study by Kaplan, a company that helps students

A Violation of the First Amendment

In 2007, a federal court ruled that the Hermitage School District in Pennsylvania violated the First Amendment free-speech rights of student Justin Layshock for punishing him for a profile he created on MySpace.

The controversy started in 2005 when Justin, along with several friends, posted parodies of his principal on MySpace. The profiles made fun of the principal and used profanity. Justin created his profile outside of school hours and off school property. When school administrators discovered the MySpace profiles, they spent a large amount of time investigating to find the creators.

When administrators identified Justin as one of the web page creators, the school punished him with a 10-day out-of-school suspension. They removed him from honors classes and placed him in an alternative curriculum education program for the remaining school year.

The ACLU of Pennsylvania filed the lawsuit on Justin's behalf. They claimed the school district's punishment for off-campus speech violated Justin's First Amendment free-speech rights.

The court agreed. "The mere fact that the internet may be accessed at school does not authorize school officials to become censors of the world wide web," U.S. District Judge Terrence McVerry said. "Public schools are vital institutions but their reach is not unlimited."[1]

1. Quoted in "Judge Finds Suspension of Student for MySpace Parody of School Principal Unconstitutional," American Civil Liberties Union of Pennsylvania, July 11, 2007. www.aclupa.org/news/2007/07/11/judge-finds-suspension-of-student-for-myspace-parody-of-school-principal-unconstitutional.

prepare for exams, found that 31 percent of college admissions staff look at candidates' social media accounts to see if the student would be a good fit for the school. The study also found that 12 percent of admissions were rejected after staff viewed their profiles.

There are some common mistakes students make that lead to their college applications being rejected. One is to make a lot of posts with foul language and pictures of themselves doing illegal or questionable things, such as posing with alcohol or drug paraphernalia. Another is posting things that contradict what they wrote in their application. For instance, if a teen writes an admissions essay about how they value academics but then tweets about hating school and wishing they could drop out, college officials are likely to assume that everything they put in their application was false.

Social Media Affects Job Prospects

Employers consider online profiles when evaluating job candidates. In one example, the president of a small consulting company in Chicago decided to check on a potential intern. On the candidate's Facebook page, the executive found descriptions of marijuana, shooting people, and other questionable things. Whether the content was truthful or just exaggeration did not matter. It landed the job seeker in the rejection pile. "A lot of it makes me think, what kind of judgment does this person have?" said Brad Karsh, the company's president. "Why are you allowing this to be viewed publicly, effectively, or semipublicly?"[61]

Karsh's company is not alone. According to a 2014 CareerBuilder survey, 43 percent of employers view candidates' social media sites, and 51 percent of those employers have rejected job candidates based on what they saw online. Michael Sciola, director of the career resource center at Wesleyan University, said, "It's a growing phenomenon. There are lots of employers that Google. Now they've taken the next step."[62] Trudy Steinfeld, executive director of the Wasserman Center for Career Development at New York University, agreed. She said, "The term they've used over and over is red flags. Is there something about their lifestyle that we might find questionable or that we might find goes against the core values of our corporation?"[63]

The CareerBuilder survey found several common reasons why employers rejected candidates:

- *Job candidate posted provocative or inappropriate photographs or information.*
- *Job candidate posted information about them drinking or using drugs.*
- *Job candidates bad-mouthed their previous company or fellow employee.*
- *Job candidate had poor communication skills.*
- *Job candidate had discriminatory comments related to race, gender, religion etc.*[64]

Some employers check candidates' social media profiles. If they find something inappropriate, it can affect their hiring decision.

However, the survey also found that candidates can use social media to present themselves in a positive light, which makes employers more likely to hire them.

Some companies purposely choose not to explore applicants' online lives. "I'd rather not see that part of them," said Maureen Crawford Hentz, manager of talent acquisition at Osram Sylvania. "I don't think it's related to their bona fide occupational qualifications."[65]

Career counselors at many colleges have advised students to review their social networking websites. They caution students to remove anything inappropriate for an audience of employers and other adults. However, whether or not the advice is being heard is unknown. "I think students have the view that Facebook is their space and that the adult world doesn't know about it," said Mark W. Smith, associate vice chancellor and director of the career center at Washington University in St. Louis. "But the adult world is starting to come in."[66]

Keeping Work and Home Lives Separate

Even for adults, the mixing of public and private worlds online can cause problems. For some users, requests from professional contacts to be friends online can be tricky. Andrew Ledbetter, assistant professor of communications studies at Ohio University in Athens, noted, "On Facebook, my high school pals, college buddies and grad school friends are lumped together with former students, current students and professional colleagues, in one big social group."[67] Ledbetter admitted that he decided not to post certain content because he believed it would not be appropriate for all of the groups in his online network.

Other users juggle the personal versus public debate by making their profiles specific to only one audience. Chuck Sanchez deleted mentions of his public relations firm on his profile. He explained, "It's simply not worth it. I want my personal site to be just that: personal."[68]

Teacher Ardath Steward used her site to keep in touch with family. However, she also made sure the content was appropriate for her middle school students to see. "There's no risky content on mine for a reason," she said. "[Being online] means anyone can see what you do. Why would I want to jeopardize my professional career?"[69]

Web Content Sticks Around

Unfortunately, cleaning up a social network profile is not as easy at it sounds. Once a photo, blog entry, or instant message is put online, users lose control. It can be printed, uploaded to other websites, and passed around in e-mail or instant messaging chains. Users cannot take it back. Suddenly, that unflattering picture is moving around the Internet indefinitely. According to Larry Rosen, professor emeritus and past chair of the Psychology Department at California State University at Dominguez Hills, users who believe they have taken the right steps to keep information private may be wrong. "It's public, whether they like it or not," he said. "And they think they can delete things, but anyone could have copied it and pasted it."[70]

As online social networks become more embedded in our society, the rules about privacy will continue to evolve. According to boyd, young people growing up in an online world no longer see privacy as keeping information confined to oneself. Instead, it has become a matter of controlling who has access. She said, "Information is not private because no one knows it; it is private because the knowing is limited and controlled."[71]

Social Media Continues to Evolve

Western society has grown increasingly wired in the last few decades. Many people appreciate the ability to share photos and posts with their friends instantly. Others worry about a loss of privacy and a decrease in people's social skills, attention spans, and problem solving abilities.

Studies into whether social media hurts or helps people have been conflicting. One 2014 study found that people who had more social connections online were more likely to get the right answers on a quiz because they were able to copy their friends. According to the website Inc, this means social networking "could be making you dumber by supplying answers and insights without requiring any actual thinking, so that your analytic powers begin to waste away like an unused muscle."[72] Another study, this one from 2013, suggested that in contrast, "social media can improve verbal, research, and critical-thinking skills, despite popular concern about the damaging effects of the internet on impressionable youths."[73]

Social media is neither good nor bad; like most things in the world, it can be either, depending on how people use it. The only thing that is certain is that it will continue to impact many areas of people's everyday lives for years to come.

Social Networking for Businesses

Shari Chiara, a marketing manager at IBM Corporation, used the company's networking site, Beehive, to check on what her coworkers were doing. Since Chiara worked from home in New York, she often felt isolated from coworkers around the world. After Beehive, "I'm more in touch with people worldwide," she said. "I'll go on and there'll be comments from people in Japan [or] Australia."[74]

Since the introduction of Beehive at IBM in 2007, more than 29,000 employees have joined the networking site. The internal site is similar to traditional social networking sites such as Facebook. It allows users to post photos and other information. Profiles can be open to the entire company or restricted to connections. "You connect with people that are further away on a more personal level,"[75] said Chiara.

Companies such as IBM, Procter and Gamble, and Nortel Networks Corporation have taken notice of the popularity of social networking and recognized a tool they can put to good use. In recent years, more employees work from home or are scattered geographically. In addition, business is more global. Customers, vendors, and consultants may work in different countries and time zones. The technology of social networking is a way to pull these groups together in a common forum. "When you have people geographically dispersed, you need to provide an interactive and immersive and intimate environment that allows them to feel communication is very natural,"[76] said Kelly Kanellakis at Nortel Networks Corporation.

Some employers feel social networks will allow employees to become more productive and work together better. "We believe innovation will happen a lot more quickly," said Kanellakis. "And because we've got such a web of communications, it'll spread a lot more quickly."[77]

LinkedIn: A Professional Social Networking Website

The growth of LinkedIn demonstrates the interest of business professionals in social networking. LinkedIn is a social network that targets career-focused, white-collar workers. LinkedIn users are generally looking to network with other professionals instead of searching for the next party. Users can post résumés online and search for experts to help solve business problems. Users link to other coworkers and business contacts, who can endorse them for certain skills. This feature shows employers that a person is being truthful on his or her résumé. Through LinkedIn, people can get introductions to more business contacts. "We want to create a broad and critical business tool that is used by tens of millions of business professionals every day to make them better at what they do,"[78] said Dan Nye, former chief executive at LinkedIn.

LINKEDIN CAN BENEFIT STUDENTS

"Actively logging on to LinkedIn made my college search easier—essentially, it streamlined the process of finding out what career to choose, and how to network with professionals. I am glad I was introduced to LinkedIn at an early age ... [It] helped me locate opportunities that I may never have thought of." —Rutha Nuguse, University of Washington freshman

Rutha Nuguse, "HS Students: Why You Need to Create a LinkedIn Profile," Youth Career Compass, www.youthcareercompass.com/networking/hs-students-why-you-need-to-create-a-linkedin-profile/

A new feature on LinkedIn, Company Groups, lets all the employees from a company on the website gather together in a private web forum. "This is a collected, protected space for employees to talk to each other and reference outside information,"[79] said Reid Hoffman, founder and chair of LinkedIn. LinkedIn believes that more companies will sign on to their site as they recognize the benefits of employees working together online. According to Jeffrey Glass, former managing director at Bain Capital and an investor in LinkedIn, "This is a powerful tool because inside the corporation, there are massive bodies of knowledge and relationships between individuals that the corporation has been unable to take advantage of until now."[80]

Many social media networks start with young adults, and the longer they are around and the more popularity they gain, the more older people start to join. With LinkedIn, this pattern was reversed. When it first started, the users of LinkedIn were older, with an average age of 41. Now, however, job experts are encouraging young people to think about their future earlier than ever. Most agree that every college student should have one, and some even feel that high school students can benefit from having a profile. Susan Adams, a contributor for *Forbes*

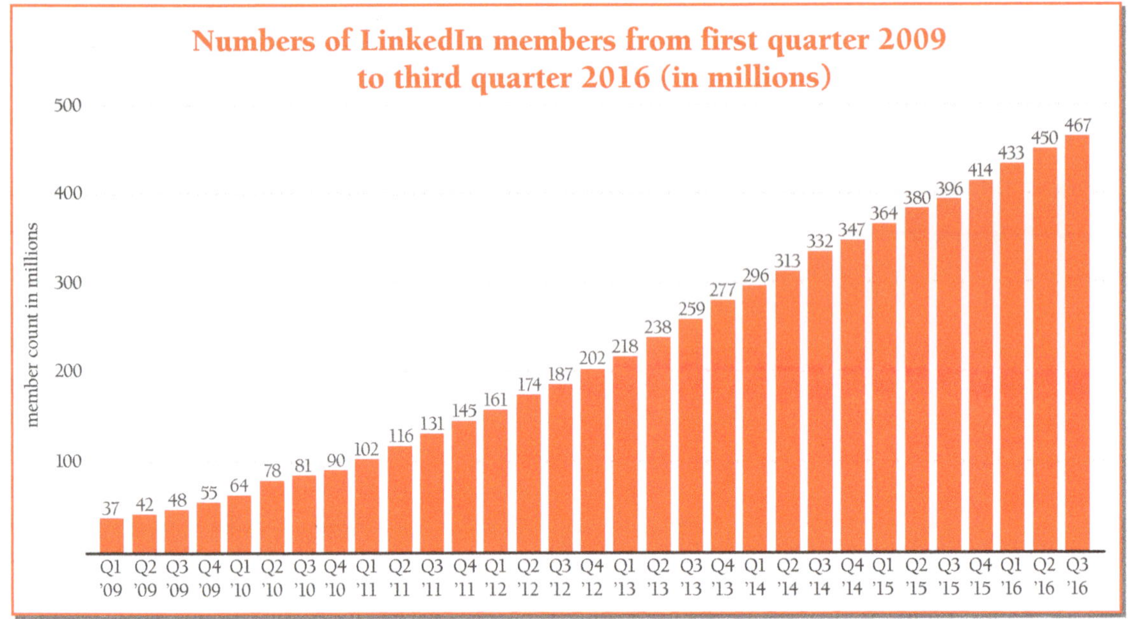

Since the beginning of 2009, 430 million people have joined LinkedIn, making it the largest professional social network to date.

magazine, believes it can improve a student's chances of getting into college. Additionally, she said,

> *If you're up for a summer job and your competition has only a resume and no LinkedIn profile, a hiring manager will likely be impressed that you have had the foresight to establish a LinkedIn presence, especially if you have several strong recommendations, more than a few endorsements, a dozen connections and a work history that shows you've held down other jobs, even if they were volunteer positions.*[81]

Adams's advice highlights the importance of being active on the website. Making a LinkedIn profile that contains nothing but a picture and the name of the school a person attends will not impress employers.

Social Media Is a Business

Social networking is also changing how businesses market their products. Text alerts, sending updates on Twitter, and creating a blog are all ways to market online. Other businesses may set up a profile page on Facebook that features pictures, reviews, and links to outside websites.

Zane Hagy owns a public relations business that uses online social networking as a core piece of his clients' marketing plans. He works on blogs for multiple clients and also sends out updates on Twitter. "There's a built-in audience, and companies are trying to figure out ways to leverage that to their advantage," he said. "There are so many different ways to put themselves in front of potential clients. It's fascinating."[82]

Suzy Trotta, a real estate agent, started a real estate blog in February 2008. She also sent out Twitter updates periodically. At first, she did not notice any substantial increase in clients. After a few months, however, she saw the momentum. "It takes awhile, but I've made connections," said Trotta. "There are those who are not ready to buy or sell yet but say they will call me because they feel like they know me and trust me."[83]

Social media marketing has become a major business. PayScale, a website that tracks the salaries of different jobs based on experience and location, reported that social media marketer was the job with the most demand for employees in 2013. Social media marketer is a title that covers a wide range of responsibilities. Just as the title "doctor" covers everything from surgeons to pediatricians, the social media marketing field can be very specialized. Job titles include search engine optimization (SEO) specialist, pay per click (PPC) specialist, and content manager. Content manager is what many people picture when they think of social media marketing—someone whose job is to post about the company on Facebook, Twitter, Instagram, and other social media sites. Many people become interested in this job because they enjoy the idea of being paid to go on social media. However, there is much more to the job than that:

> *Effective social media marketers are successful at gauging the marketplace, generating buzz-worthy content, expanding the company's reach, engaging with audiences across various platforms, and being attentive to what the community is asking for and saying. Additionally, they are also responsible for creating, implementing, and managing various social marketing campaigns for companies.*[84]

Being a content manager can be difficult because they need to make sure the things they post get a lot of attention. If a post does not get a lot of likes or retweets, the marketer needs to figure out a better way to catch people's attention. They must also be very careful not to offend anyone with their posts, as this can damage the company's reputation.

Companies on Twitter

Twitter is a popular social networking site both for individuals and businesses. Most companies today have a Twitter account to promote their products and services. They can also connect with industry professionals, keep up to date on trends, and share ideas. "Where Twitter is cool is that you're able to see what people are working on. It's a tool to bring more people into your life, whether personally or professionally, and to get your voice heard,"[1] explained Al Krueger, founder of a strategic branding and public relations firm.

However, just like individuals, companies need to be careful what they say on social media. Offensive or ignorant tweets are often screenshotted and shared over and over again in articles and on TV. For instance, in 2016, MTV Australia tweeted that it needed English subtitles to understand actresses America Ferrera and Eva Longoria at the Golden Globes. Outraged viewers criticized MTV Australia for its racist remark. The company apologized twice, but the damage was done.

1. Quoted in Tannette Johnson-Elie, "Twitter Blends Online Networking, Instant Messaging," *Milwaukee Journal Sentinel*, June 24, 2008. www.jsonline.com/story/index.aspx?id=765641.

Increasing Voter Turnout

The 2008 U.S. presidential primaries and election ushered social networking into the political spotlight. According to a Pew Research Center study, 46 percent of Americans used the Internet to get news about the campaign or share their opinions on the candidates. This was a significant increase from the 31 percent who used the Internet at the same point in the 2004 election. The Pew study also found that 35 percent of Americans had watched campaign videos online. In addition, 40 percent of Americans with social networking profiles—10 percent of all Americans—used social networking websites for political reasons. Young adults drove this surge in online political activity. The study found that half of all young adults with social networking profiles used these sites to research candidates or volunteer for a campaign.

Barack Obama, who was an Illinois senator at the time, used websites and social networking tools to connect with voters during his presidential campaign. His team designed a site that was similar to Facebook. On MyBarackObama.com, supporters could join local groups, organize events, and read the campaign's blog.

When Barack Obama was campaigning for president, he used social media tools to connect with voters.

People also used the site to donate to Obama's campaign, raising millions of dollars from everyday Americans. Obama himself saw social networking as key to his campaign. "One of my fundamental beliefs from my days as a community organizer is that real change comes from the bottom up," he said in a statement. "And there's no more powerful tool for grass-roots organizing than the Internet."[85]

Another 2008 presidential candidate, Ron Paul, was relatively unknown prior to his campaign. Through the efforts of grassroots supporters online, the Paul campaign raised a record $4 million in a single day. A few weeks later, the campaign broke its own record and raised over $6 million in a 24-hour period. Paul supporters were active on blogs, online polls, and social networks. While other candidates had more money and the support of the major political parties, Paul proved that an active online community can launch a lesser-known candidate into the spotlight. The low-cost Internet may become a way for future political candidates to bring their message to the public without the financial backing of the major political parties.

The success of Obama's and Paul's social networking strategies sparked interest from other political candidates. "Their use of social networks will guide the way for future campaigns,"[86] said Peter Daou, digital media strategist for Hillary Clinton's 2008 presidential primary campaign. Candidates have realized the importance of social networking to their campaigns. According to Alan Rosenblatt, a blogger at TechPresident, the example set by the 2008 campaign sends a clear message. "Not only do voters use the Internet to learn about the candidates and the issues, but they are sharing it with others," he said. "This is most important. It means that what people learn on the Internet influences nearly everyone in the country."[87]

The Problem of Sharing Fake News

Continuing this trend, social media also played a significant part in the 2016 U.S. presidential election. Candidates continued to use Facebook, Twitter, and campaign websites to broadcast their views. Donald Trump, in particular, drew attention for how often he used Twitter to post things that many people considered offensive or that were later proven to be factually incorrect. This behavior led his campaign staff to take over his Twitter account for several days before the election. Hillary Clinton also came under fire because in the past, she had sent government e-mails through her private e-mail account. Many people were worried that because her personal e-mail was less secure, government secrets could be stolen by hackers. Clinton was investigated and cleared of wrongdoing, but her e-mail use remained a major focus of the election.

After Donald Trump's victory was announced, people began to realize that false news reports circulated on social media played a part in Trump's victory. People tend to share articles without reading anything more than the title, so online news outlets often make a title intentionally misleading to encourage more people to share it because shares, likes, and views increase a company's ratings. The practice of making misleading or vague titles to get someone to view an article is called "clickbait." In one example, *Morning News USA* wrote an article entitled, "Hillary Clinton Quotes: Nurses are Overpaid Maids, Glorified Babysitters." People who did not read the actual article were angry about this and shared it on social media to encourage other people not to vote for Clinton. The article itself noted several times that there was no proof Clinton had ever said such a thing, but many people took the title as truth.

Researchers also found after the election that the Russian government had "created and spread misleading articles online with the goal of punishing Democrat Hillary Clinton, helping Republican Donald Trump and undermining faith in American democracy."[88] It is unclear whether these tactics were responsible for Trump's win, but

Russian President Vladimir Putin was accused of ordering the spreading of fake news online.

they certainly cast doubt on the trustworthiness of American news sources.

The problem of fake news is not limited to politics or other serious topics. All kinds of rumors are spread through social media. For instance, in 2014, a text photo went viral on Facebook. It claimed that Facebook was starting a "No Swearing" campaign and that anyone who used swear words in their posts would be locked out of their account or banned permanently. Many people shared the photo because they were angry that Facebook would try to limit their right to free speech. In reality, the message was completely fake.

In a time where anyone can post anything on the Internet, it is very important for people to research what they see before reposting. Some fake news is harmless, while other stories can have a serious impact. Sites such as Facebook, Google, and Twitter have promised to try to delete fake news when they find it, but it is impossible for them to catch it all. Therefore, it is up to the user to evaluate what he or she sees. Some tips to figure out whether an item is fake or not include:

- A title is in all capital letters or includes a picture that is obviously Photoshopped.
- The website has a lot of popup or banner ads.
- The URL is almost—but not exactly—the same as a legitimate website.
- The "About" section on an unknown website is vague or contains errors.
- Googling an unknown website along with the word "fake" shows multiple results.
- Links in an article lead to untrustworthy websites, or there are no links or quotes at all.
- No other websites are reporting the same story.
- The article is years out of date.

- The article contradicts the headline.
- Dragging and dropping suspicious pictures into Google Images shows that the original location of the photo is a completely different article.

If a story seems purposely offensive, it is probably designed to make people angry enough to share without fact checking. It is also a good idea to check the website Snopes if an article seems suspicious. The researchers at this website look into Internet rumors to see if they are true, partially true, or outright false.

Social Networking for Churches

Social networks are also expanding into churches. Christian leaders recognize that social networks allow them to keep in touch more effectively with youth ministry, college groups, and other church groups. Dale Tadlock is the associate pastor of a Baptist church. He uses Facebook to keep in touch with the young people at his church and send out event reminders. "It has given me a great opportunity to work with students," he said. "It's become a way to stay informed."[89]

CHANGES FOR CHURCHES

"I think it's just changed the way we are interacting and the way we are doing things. I think it literally has changed our culture."
–Dale Tadlock, associate pastor of the First Baptist Church of Waynesboro, Virginia

Quoted in Rachel Mehlhaff, "Jesus in MySpace: Churches Use Social-Networking Sites," *Associated Baptist Press*, July 3, 2008. www.abpnews.com/index.php?option=com_content&task=view&id=3392&Itemid=53.

Other churches choose to join OnFaith, a social networking site built for congregations. The website is not limited to Christians; anyone of any faith can join. OnFaith users can send messages to specific users or to groups. They announce prayer requests and advertise events. They also use the website to share photos, audio files, and comments on sermons.

Volunteer Opportunities Online

In past generations, people who were passionate about a cause relied on word of mouth, paper flyers, and face-to-face club meetings to spread the news about their activities. Today, more people turn to the Internet for information about volunteering and social causes. Online, organizations for social causes can set up profiles and quickly gather thousands of followers. The website Volunteer Match allows people to set a location and either search for a specific type of activity or browse what is available in their area. Organizations can post volunteer openings so people will be able to find them.

Individual activists can decorate their profiles with photos of volunteer events and write blogs about their efforts. They can send e-mails in support of a cause to politicians, corporate executives, or newspaper editors.

Getting the word out about the latest event or rally is as easy as sending an e-mail, text alert, or profile update. In 2006, more than 100,000 students in a California public school district skipped class on May 1 in support of immigration rights. Many of the students learned about the protest and the immigration issue through comments and pages on MySpace.

Social Media for Celebrities

Other groups, such as libraries and authors, use social networking to advertise programs and book launches. Libraries with profiles on Facebook and MySpace communicate with users on the latest news and programs through profile entries. Blogs allow authors to update readers with the latest information on appearances, readings, or television interviews.

Author Marcy Dermansky used her MySpace page and its Top 8 Friends list feature to promote her novel. All eight of her "friends" had the same names as the characters in her book. She searched the website for people with the needed names, including some unusual ones like Yumiko and Smita, and

Justin Timberlake is one celebrity who often answers his fans on Twitter.

approached them with her idea. Some were so receptive they ended up buying her book to learn more about their character.

Dermansky believed that using MySpace to promote her book helped increase sales and improve her name recognition as an author. She also believed that the site helped her to be more accessible to readers. "It's intimidating to write a fan letter to an author. There is the fear of being dorky or inarticulate. But in the MySpace universe, somehow that kind of inhibition and difficulty has been broken down,"[90] she said.

Many social media websites have opened up that kind of availability to celebrities, but none more so than Twitter. Although many celebrities have Facebook pages, the posts are often made by social media marketing staff to promote their work. On Twitter, however, celebrities can have their own accounts and typically tweet their own thoughts. They may not see every tweet they are tagged in, but if one catches their eye, they can and often do respond.

People love the idea of celebrities responding to them so much that comedian Jimmy Kimmel created a very popular segment on his show, *Jimmy Kimmel Live*. The segment is called "Celebrities Read Mean Tweets," where Kimmel films celebrities reading insulting tweets about themselves out loud and then responding to the people who wrote them.

Personalized Social Networks

Some services, such as Ning, allow users to create their own social networks. Users can customize the network to focus on their own specific interests, companies, fans, and friends. Artists, athletes, journalists, students, parents, crafters, and special interest groups all have created social networks through Ning. Marc Andreessen, cofounder of Ning, believes in the appeal of custom networks. "The existing social networks are fantastic but they put users in a straitjacket … they were not built to be flexible," he said. "They do not let people build and design their own worlds, which is the nature of what people want to do online."[91]

As more social networks spring up, it will be inconvenient for users to enter the same information into multiple sites. A megasite or another way to transfer information between

Sports Teams Join Social Media

The Washington Glory, a former professional softball team, demonstrated how lesser-known sports teams can use social networks to build a fan base. The team signed up for a MySpace page in 2007. Owner Paul Wilson used the site to send out coupons for discounted admissions to games and respond to messages from fans. Whenever he saw a young person thanking a player for answering his or her online message, he knew the site was working. "Now they communicate so much through online or text messages," said Wilson. "So instead of getting them to come to us, I wanted to go to them."[1]

Because social network advertising is free, teams in less popular professional leagues can afford the online promotion. Lacking national exposure, these teams frequently target a niche market. Online media provides the perfect opportunity to reach potential fans successfully.

1. Quoted in Mark Viera, "Befriending Generation Facebook," *Washington Post*, July 15, 2008. www.washingtonpost.com/wp-dyn/content/article/2008/07/14/AR2008071402144.html.

websites appears to be inevitable. Marc Canter supports OpenID, a project that would let users easily transfer profile information among several social networks. "Humans are migratory beasts, and we do not want to re-enter our data every time we join a new site," he said. "Users own their data and should be able to move it around freely."[92]

International Messaging Apps

As smartphones play an increasingly large role in people's daily lives, they want to be connected to friends and family no matter where they are in the world. Apps such as WhatsApp, Telegram, and Facebook Messenger use a phone's data plan rather than text messaging, so messages can be sent over the Internet. Since many texting plans do not work between countries, this allows people to stay in touch when they are traveling. Additionally, for immigrants who move to a new country, these messaging apps can offer them an easy way to stay in touch with friends and

International messaging apps help people keep in touch no matter where they are in the world.

family members they left behind. Some people also prefer these apps because they make sending photos and videos much easier than texting does.

TAKE A BREAK

"We are not [robots] that can stay connected to the Internet, gleefully task switching for hours on end without breaks, and expect ourselves to not feel anxiety about missing out on something that 'might' happen when we are disconnected ... Practice doing something to calm your brain every 90 minutes and perhaps you will avoid that [fear of missing out] feeling." –Larry Rosen, research psychologist

Larry Rosen, "Always On, All the Time. Are We Suffering from FoMO?," *Psychology Today*, May 2, 2013. www.psychologytoday.com/blog/rewired-the-psychology-technology/201305/always-all-the-time-are-we-suffering-fomo.

Changes in Society

As more people embrace social networks, the line between the online world and the world outside the Internet will start to fade. In many cases, social networks and online activity have already impacted how people interact with each other and behave away from their computers.

Professionally, social networks foster collaboration among spread-out groups. Before, it was difficult and expensive to share information and ideas with people in different geographic locations. Using social networks, scientists share details on research projects and get input from colleagues around the world. Teachers gather to share ideas and projects for the classroom. Even businesspeople can turn online for solutions to common company problems with vendors, customers, and employees.

Social networks also impact the ways in which people interact with each other on a personal level. Before social networks, people engaged in hours of small talk to learn each other's favorite foods, movies, and pet peeves. Over time, they revealed details about their own life, family, and emotions.

Now, users can search online for people they have just met. Suddenly, there is no need for hours of small talk. Users can learn all about a new friend just by reading their social network profile. Some of this research occurs even before people meet in person. By researching online, many people discover the personal details about a casual acquaintance that used to be knowledge reserved for close friends.

What Happens to a Profile When Someone Dies?

Many young people have found that social networks give them a comfortable place to express their feelings about the passing of a friend or family member. When 23-year-old Deborah Lee Walker died in an automobile accident, her father logged on to her MySpace page and found many messages from friends expressing sorrow over her death.

Some people keep their loved one's profile active after they die, turning it into an online memorial for that person. Reading messages and visiting the page of a deceased friend or loved one can provide comfort. "I still believe that even though she's not the one on her MySpace page, that's a way I can reach out to her," said Jenna Finke about a friend who died. "Her really close friends go on there every day. It means a lot to know people aren't forgetting her."[93]

Others are disturbed by the public nature of what has traditionally been a private matter. Some families can become overwhelmed by messages from strangers. In some cases, they reach out to the families for help in dealing with their own loss. To Walker's mother, these messages were not welcome: "The grief of our own friends and family is almost more than we can bear on top of our own, and we don't need anyone else's on our shoulders."[94]

Predicting the Future

Before social networking, many people primarily interacted with others in the same community and nearby regions. Often, phone calls and travel to faraway places were too expensive to keep up regular contact. For many people, letters to a pen pal were the only contact they had with a person from another country.

Now, with the widespread availability of computers and the Internet, everyday citizens are able to connect with people across the world on a regular basis. It is as easy to talk online with a friend in India as one who lives across the street. Users might initially find each other through a shared interest or hobby. That initial contact may gradually lead to more conversations and understanding about different cultures, languages, and experiences. In this way, some people believe that social networking will bring people together in a global community. They feel the technology will break down geographical and political barriers.

Besides the ever-expanding groups of new users online, the way in which people experience social networks will also evolve. It is difficult to predict exactly what new kinds of social media websites will spring up in the future, but researchers have been looking at trends in order to do just that. New types of social media are springing up all the time, but what remains to be seen is whether or not they will explode in popularity the way sites such as Facebook, Pinterest, Instagram, and YouTube have.

Currently, it seems as though live video streaming is gaining popularity. Since 2015, multiple live streaming websites and apps have been launched, including Meerkat, Periscope, and YouNow. YouNow, especially, is quickly growing in popularity. Users can pay to watch others act, sing, sleep, or talk to each other. Because of this payment, the app does not need ads. Facebook has also added a live streaming feature to keep up with the times.

It is not possible to know exactly how social networking will change in the future. The only thing that can be said for certain is that it will continue to impact people's lives. Social networking has become a natural extension of human interaction, similar to the telephone and e-mail. It will continue to grow, evolve, and become more easily accessible as technology advances.

NOTES

Introduction: Social Networking: An Overview

1. Quoted in Carol Brydolf, "Minding MySpace: Balancing the Benefits and Risks of Students' Online Social Networks," *Education Digest*, October 2007. www.csba.org/NewsAndMedia/Publications/CASchoolsMagazine/2007/Spring/InThisIssue/Minding_MySpace.aspx.

2. Quoted in Anthony Williams, "Area Teachers Made Examples of What Not to Do Online," *Houston Chronicle*, June 30, 2008. www.chron.com/neighborhood/memorial-news/article/Area-teachers-made-examples-of-what-not-to-do-1621786.php.

3. Quoted in Brydolf, "Minding MySpace."

Chapter 1: The History of Social Networking

4. Quoted in Patricia Sellers, "MySpace Cowboys," *Fortune*, September 4, 2006. money.cnn.com/magazines/fortune/fortune_archive/2006/09/04/8384727/index.htm.

5. Quoted in Sellers, "MySpace Cowboys."

6. Alek, interview with author, December 20, 2016.

7. Quoted in Alex Wright, "Friending, Ancient or Otherwise," *New York Times*, December 2, 2007. www.nytimes.com/2007/12/02/weekinreview/02wright.html.

8. Quoted in Wright, "Friending, Ancient or Otherwise."

9. Quoted in Wright, "Friending, Ancient or Otherwise."

Chapter 2: How Social Networking Changed Everyday Life

10. Uptin Saiidi, "Social Media Making Millennials Less Social: Study," CNBC, October 17, 2015. www.cnbc.com/2015/10/15/social-media-making-millennials-less-social-study.html.

11. Larry Rosen and Keith N. Hampton, "Is Technology Making People Less Sociable?" *The Wall Street Journal*, May 10, 2015. www.wsj.com/articles/is-technology-making-people-less-sociable-1431093491.

12. Quoted in Larry Magid and Anne Collier, *MySpace Unraveled: A Parent's Guide to Teen Social Networking*. Berkeley, CA: Peachpit, 2007, p. 16.

13. Quoted in Connie Neal, *MySpace for Moms and Dads*. Grand Rapids, MI: Zondervan, 2007, p. 29.

14. Quoted in Anastasia Goodstein, *Totally Wired: What Teens and Tweens Are Really Doing Online*. New York, NY: St. Martin's, 2007, p. 22.

15. Amanda Lenhart, "Teens, Technology and Friendships," Pew Research Center, August 06, 2015. www.pewinternet.org/2015/08/06/teens-technology-and-friendships/.

16. Quoted in Candice M. Kelsey, *Generation MySpace: Helping Your Teen Survive Online Adolescence*. New York, NY: Marlowe, 2007, p. 14.

17. A. Pawlowski, "Secret Life of Teens: Internet Addiction Changes Boy into 'Shell of a Son,'" *Today*, September 18, 2014. www.today.com/parents/secret-life-teens-internet-addiction-changes-boy-shell-son-1D80153806.

18. Quoted in Hattie Kauffman, "Social Networking: An Internet Addiction," CBSNews.com, June 24, 2008. www.cbsnews.com/stories/2008/06/24/earlyshow/main4205009.shtml?source=search_story.

19. danah boyd, "Blame Society, Not the Screen Time," *New York Times*, July 11, 2016. www.nytimes.com/roomfordebate/2015/07/16/is-internet-addiction-a-health-threat-for-teenagers/blame-society-not-the-screen-time.

20. Nancy Jo Sales, "Social Media and Secret Lives of American Girls," *TIME*, 2016. time.com/americangirls/.

21. Quoted in Robin M. Lowalski, Susan P. Limber, and Patricia W. Agatston, *Cyber Bullying*. Maldon, MA: Blackwell, 2008, p. 42.

22. danah boyd, *It's Complicated: The Social Lives of Networked Teens*. New Haven, CT: Yale University Press, 2014, p. 131.

23. Quoted in Kelsey, *Generation MySpace*, p. 111.

24. Quoted in Nancy Jo Sales, "Friends Without Benefits," *Vanity Fair*, September 26, 2013. www.vanityfair.com/news/2013/09/social-media-internet-porn-teenage-girls.

25. Quoted in Kelsey, *Generation MySpace*, p. 120.

26. Magid and Collier, *MySpace Unraveled*, p. 12.

Chapter 3: Staying Safe on the Internet

27. Quoted in Rob Stafford, "Why Parents Must Mind MySpace," MSNBC.com, April 5, 2006. www.msnbc.msn.com/ed/11064451.

28. Quoted in Julie Steenhuysen, "Study Rejects Internet Sex Predator Stereotype," Reuters, February 18, 2008. www.reuters.com/article/us-sex-predator-idUSN1560642020080218.

29. Quoted in Steenhuysen, "Study Rejects Internet Sex Predator Stereotype."

30. Quoted in Steenhuysen, "Study Rejects Internet Sex Predator Stereotype."

31. Quoted in Cindy Long, "I Need My Space!" *NEA Today*, April 2007. www.nea.org/home/11405.htm.

32. Quoted in Steenhuysen, "Study Rejects Internet Sex Predator Stereotype."

33. Julia Glum, "Online Safety For Teens: Are Internet Friends A Good Thing?" *International Business Times*, August 14, 2015. www.ibtimes.com/online-safety-teens-are-internet-friends-good-thing-2052238.

34. Quoted in Kelsey, *Generation MySpace*, p. 174.

35. Sales, "Friends Without Benefits."

36. Quoted in Sales, "Friends Without Benefits."

37. Quoted in Sales, "Friends Without Benefits."

38. Quoted in Kate Fillion, "Problems Happen in Any Community. The Sense MySpace Is Where All These Bad Things Are Happening Is Overblown," *Maclean's*, May 14, 2007. www.macleans.ca/article.jsp?content=20070514_105154_105154.

39. Emil Protalinski, "Facebook Scans Chats and Posts for Criminal Activity," CNET, July 12, 2012. www.cnet.com/news/facebook-scans-chats-and-posts-for-criminal-activity/.

40. danah boyd and Henry Jenkins, "MySpace and Deleting Online Predators Act (DOPA)," MIT Tech Talk, May 26, 2006. www.danah.org/papers/MySpaceDOPA.html.

41. Quoted in Tara Bahrampour and Lori Aratani, "Teens' Bold Blogs Alarm Area Schools," *Washington Post*, January 17, 2006. www.washingtonpost.com/wp-dyn/content/article/2006/01/16/AR2006011601489_2.html.

42. boyd and Jenkins, "MySpace and Deleting Online Predators Act (DOPA)."

43. Quoted in Goodstein, *Totally Wired*, p. 104.

Chapter 4: Privacy on the Internet

44. Quoted in Tara Bahrampour, "On the Web, 'Dear Diary' Becomes 'Dear World,'" *Washington Post*, January 7, 2007. www.washingtonpost.com/wp-dyn/content/article/ 2007/01/01/AR2007010100758.html.

45. Quoted in Bahrampour, "On the Web, 'Dear Diary' Becomes 'Dear World.'"

46. Quoted in Bahrampour, "On the Web, 'Dear Diary' Becomes 'Dear World.'"

47. Quoted in Amanda Lenhart and Mary Madden, "Teens, Privacy & Online Social Networks," Pew Research Center, April 18, 2007. www.pewinternet.org/2007/04/18/online-privacy-what-teens-share-and-restrict-in-an-online-environment/.

48. Quoted in Lenhart and Madden, "Teens, Privacy & Online Social Networks."

49. Quoted in Lenhart and Madden, "Teens, Privacy & Online Social Networks."

50. Quoted in Martha Irvine, "Privacy Becomes Concern as Social Online Sites Become Fair Game," *USA Today*, December 30, 2006. www.usatoday.com/tech/news/2006-12-30 privacy-online_x.htm.

51. boyd, *It's Complicated: The Social Lives of Networked Teens.*

52. Quoted in Martha Irvine, "Online Privacy More Complicated than It Seems," *Courant*, June 22, 2008. www.courant.com/features/lifestyle/hc-privacy.artjun22, 0,1782562.story.

53. Quoted in Kim Hart, "A Flashy Facebook Page, at a Cost to Privacy," *Washington Post*, June 12, 2008. www.washingtonpost.com/wpdyn/content/article/2008/06/11/AR2008 061103759.html.

54. Quoted in Goodstein, *Totally Wired*, p. 36.

55. Quoted in Lenhart and Madden, "Teens, Privacy & Online Social Networks."

56. Quoted in Lenhart and Madden, "Teens, Privacy & Online Social Networks."

57. Quoted in Bahrampour and Aratani, "Teens' Bold Blogs Alarm Area Schools."

58. Quoted in Bahrampour and Aratani, "Teens' Bold Blogs Alarm Area Schools."

59. Quoted in Janet Kornblum and Mary Beth Marklein, "What You Say Online Could Haunt You," *USA Today*, March 8, 2006. www.usatoday.com/tech/news/internetprivacy/2006-03-08-facebook-myspace_x.htm.

60. Quoted in Kornblum and Marklein, "What You Say Online Could Haunt You."

61. Quoted in Alan Finder, "For Some, Online Persona Undermines a Resume," *New York Times*, June 11, 2006. www.nytimes.com/2006/06/11/us/11recruit.html.

62. Quoted in Finder, "For Some, Online Persona Undermines a Resume."

63. Quoted in Finder, "For Some, Online Persona Undermines a Resume."

64. "Number of Employers Passing on Applicants Due to Social Media Posts Continues to Rise, According to New CareerBuilder Survey," CareerBuilder, June 26, 2014. www.careerbuilder.com/share/aboutus/pressreleasesdetail.aspx?sd=6%2F26%2F2014&id=pr829&ed=12%2F31%2F2014.

65. Quoted in Finder, "For Some, Online Persona Undermines a Resume."

66. Quoted in Finder, "For Some, Online Persona Undermines a Resume."

67. Quoted in Janet Kornblum, "Social, Work Lives Collide on Networking Websites," *USA Today*, January 18, 2008. www.usatoday.com/tech/webguide/internetlife/2008-01-17-social-network-nobarriers_N.htm.

68. Quoted in Irvine, "Privacy Becomes Concern as Social Online Sites Become Fair Game."

69. Quoted in Williams, "Area Teachers Made Examples of What Not to Do Online."

70. Quoted in Williams, "Area Teachers Made Examples of What Not to Do Online."

71. Quoted in Ari Melber, "About Facebook," *Nation*, January 7–14, 2008. www.thenation.com/doc/20080107/melber.

Chapter 5: Social Networking Continues to Evolve

72. Jessica Stillman, "Social Media Is Making You Stupid," Inc, February 20, 2014. www.inc.com/jessica-stillman/social-media-is-making-you-stupid.html.

73. Monica Nickelsburg, "Does Social Media Make Us Smarter?" *The Week*, September 17, 2013. theweek.com/articles/459968/does-social-media-make-smarter.

74. Quoted in Barbara Rose, "Social Networks Link Workers," *Chicago Tribune*, June 17, 2008. www.chicagotribune.com/business/chi-tue-corporate-social-networkjun17,0,1112300.story.

75. Quoted in Rose, "Social Networks Link Workers."

76. Quoted in Rose, "Social Networks Link Workers."

77. Quoted in Rose, "Social Networks Link Workers."

78. Quoted in Brad Stone, "At Social Site, Only the Businesslike Need Apply," *New York Times*, June 18, 2008. www.nytimes.com/2008/06/18/technology/18linkedin.html?_r=1&scp=1&sq=At%20Social%20Site,%20Only%20the%20Busi nesslike%20Need%20Apply&st=cse.

79. Quoted in Stone, "At Social Site, Only the Businesslike Need Apply."

80. Quoted in Stone, "At Social Site, Only the Businesslike Need Apply."

81. Susan Adams, "Eight Reasons High School Students Should Be on LinkedIn," *Forbes*, May 14, 2013. www.forbes.com/sites/susanadams/2013/05/14/eight-reasons-high-school-students-should-be-on-linkedin/.

82. Quoted in Carly Harrington, "All a Twitter: Businesses Keyed Up About Using Social Networking to Create Relationships with Customers," *Knoxville News Sentinel*, June 15, 2008. www.knoxnews.com/news/2008/Jun/15/all-a-twitter/.

83. Quoted in Harrington, "All a Twitter."

84. Leah Arnold-Smeets, "Social Media Marketer—Most In-Demand Job Skill of 2013," PayScale, January 7, 2014. www.payscale.com/career-news/2014/01/social-media-marketer-most-in-demand-job-skill-of-2013.

85. Quoted in Brian Stelter, "Obama Harnesses Power of Web Social Networking," *Seattle Times*, July 7, 2008. seattletimes.nwsource.com/html/politics/2008036639_obamaface 07.html.

86. Quoted in Stelter, "Obama Harnesses Power of Web Social Networking."

87. Quoted in Heather Havenstein, "Web Use in 2008 Political Campaigns Shattering Records in U.S.," Computerworld, June 18, 2008. www.computerworld.com/action/article.do?command=viewArticleBasic&articleId=9100038.

88. Craig Timberg, "Russian Propaganda Effort Helped Spread 'Fake News' During Election, Experts Say," *Washington Post*, November 24, 2016. www.washingtonpost.com/business/economy/russian-propaganda-effort-helped-spread-fake-news-during-election-experts-say/2016/11/24/793903b6-8a40-4ca9-b712-716af66098fe_story.html?utm_term=.1f09e428404e.

89. Quoted in Rachel Mehlhaff, "Jesus in MySpace: Churches Use Social-Networking Sites," *Associated Baptist Press*, July 3, 2008. www.abpnews.com/index.php?option=com_content&task=view&id=3392&Itemid=53.

90. Quoted in Rachel Kramer Bussel, "How Many Friends Does Your Book Have?" Mediabistro.com, August 7, 2006. www.mediabistro.com/articles/cache/a8194.asp.

91. Quoted in Brad Stone, "Social Networking's Next Phase," *New York Times*, March 3, 2007. www.nytimes.com/2007/03/03/technology/03social.html.

92. Quoted in Stone, "Social Networking's Next Phase."

93. Quoted in Warren St. John, "Rituals of Grief Go Online," *New York Times*, April 27, 2006. www.nytimes.com/2006/04/27/technology/27myspace.html.

94. Quoted in St. John, "Rituals of Grief Go Online."

DISCUSSION QUESTIONS

Chapter 1: The History of Social Networking

1. What factors influenced the rise of social networking?
2. Do you use social media? Why or why not?
3. What are the differences between open and closed social networks? Which one do you feel is better?

Chapter 2: How Social Networking Changed Everyday Life

1. Does social networking make people more or less social? Give examples to support your answer.
2. What are the benefits and drawbacks to social networking?
3. Why does cyberbullying impact victims in a more personal and relentless way than traditional bullying?

Chapter 3: Staying Safe on the Internet

1. Is banning social networking sites entirely an appropriate and effective way to keep users safe?
2. What measures should users take to ensure personal safety on social networking sites?
3. What are the challenges governments and schools face when trying to regulate the Internet?

Chapter 4: Privacy on the Internet

1. How has the meaning of personal privacy changed since the introduction of social networks?
2. What kind of information is okay to share publicly? What kind of information should be kept private?
3. As more people move online, what conflicts may arise between personal and public lives?

Chapter 5: Social Networking Continues to Evolve

1. In what ways is social networking part of people's everyday lives?
2. In what ways does social networking change human behavior? Are these changes desirable?
3. How is social networking bringing the world closer together?

ORGANIZATIONS TO CONTACT

American Civil Liberties Union (ACLU)
125 Broad Street
18th Floor
New York, NY 10004
Phone: (212) 549-2500
Website: www.aclu.org
The ACLU is a nonprofit organization that believes civil liberties must be respected, even in times of national emergency. The ACLU has been active in several cases involving free-speech rights and social networking. It has an affiliate in every state and Puerto Rico, which can be contacted through the ACLU website.

Child Exploitation Investigations Unit
Phone: (866) 347-2423 (1-866-DHS-2ICE)
Website: www.ice.gov/predator
This branch of U.S. Immigration and Customs Enforcement (ICE) encourages people to call its toll-free hotline if they or someone they know is being targeted by a child predator.

National Suicide Prevention Lifeline
Phone: (800) 273-8255 (800-273-TALK)
Website: www.suicidepreventionlifeline.org
This service provides free, confidential crisis support for anyone who is considering suicide for any reason. A live chat is also available through the website.

STOMP Out Bullying
Phone: (877) 602-8559 (877-NOBULLY)
Website: www.stompoutbullying.org
This organization is dedicated to stopping bullying and cyberbullying by raising awareness. The website includes a free,

confidential live chat for anyone over the age of 13 who needs to speak to an adult about bullying.

The Trevor Project
Phone (Lifeline): (866) 488-7386 (866-4-U-TREVOR)
Text: (202) 304-1200
Website: www.thetrevorproject.org
LGBT young adults experience bullying at higher rates than cisgender young adults. Anyone who has been the target of bullying because of their sexual orientation can contact The Trevor Project. The Lifeline is available 24 hours a day, 7 days a week for people who need to talk to a crisis intervention counselor immediately. A live chat is available on the website every day between 3:00 p.m. and 9:00 p.m. Eastern Standard Time (EST), and counselors are available via text on Thursdays and Fridays between 4:00 p.m. and 8:00 p.m. EST.

FOR MORE INFORMATION

Books

Birley, Shane. *How to Be a Blogger and Vlogger in 10 Easy Lessons.* Lake Forest, CA: Walter Foster Jr., 2016.
Blogging and vlogging (video blogging) are fast-growing career fields. More than one individual has been signed to a book or video deal after he or she started a blog or vlog. Young adults can learn how to break into this field and share their talents with the world in a safe, effective way.

Head, Honor. *How to Handle Cyberbullying.* Mankato, MN: Smart Apple Media, 2015.
Cyberbullying is a serious problem that can have devastating effects on the victim's mental health. Learning how to deal with cyberbullying before it happens can help young adults feel more in control of the situation if it arises.

Klipper, Barbara, Rhonda Shapiro-Rieser, and Yasmin Bahrami. *The Secret Rules of Social Networking.* Lenexa, KS: AAPC Publishing, 2015.
Navigating social situations in person can be difficult, but social media websites have their own type of etiquette. This guide to being social online explains what is and is not considered appropriate when it comes to friending or following someone, commenting on posts, and keeping communication private.

Minton, Eric. *Social Networking and Social Media Safety.* New York, NY: PowerKids Press, 2014.
This book teaches the basics of what should and should not be put on a social media profile, how to create an uncrackable password, and how to use privacy settings.

Mozer, Mindy. *A Teen's Guide to the Power of Social Networking: Social Network-Powered Education Opportunities.* New York, NY: Rosen Publishing, 2014.
Social media can be used for much more than sharing photos and liking posts. Mozer discusses how young adults can use social media to find volunteer opportunities, bring awareness to issues such as racism and sexism, and affect local and national policy.

Websites

ConnectSafely
www.connectsafely.org
ConnectSafely is for parents, teens, educators, and advocates interested in the impact of the social web. The website has tips for teens and parents and resources for safe blogging and social networking.

NetSmartz
www.netsmartz.org/Teens
This website, run by the National Center for Missing and Exploited Children, gives tips for using social media safely and minimizing online drama. The website includes a cyber tipline for teens to report someone who is sexually harassing them or their friends online.

Snopes
www.snopes.com
A reputable source of information staffed by researchers, Snopes can help people find out if news stories and rumors are fact or fiction.

Volunteer Match
www.volunteermatch.org
Use the power of social networking to find ways to help in the local community.

WiredSafety
www.wiredsafety.org
WiredSafety is a nonprofit group that provides help, information, and education for Internet and mobile device users of all ages.

INDEX

W

Y

Z

PICTURE CREDITS

Cover junpinzon/Shutterstock.com; pp. 7, 27 Rawpixel.com/Shutterstock.com; p. 8 sturti/E+/Getty Images; p. 11 360b/Shutterstock.com; p. 14 Gil C/Shutterstock.com; p. 16 Adrian Brown/Bloomberg via Getty Images; p. 29 antoniodiaz/Shutterstock.com; p. 32 Creatas Images/Creatas/Thinkstock; p. 34 Photographee.eu/Shutterstock.com; p. 37 Tibrina Hobson/WireImage/Getty Images; p. 40 DGLimages/iStock/Thinkstock; p. 42 Photo Works/Shutterstock.com; p. 46 Michael Nigro/Pacific Press/LightRocket via Getty Images; p. 51 ERIC FEFERBERG/AFP/Getty Images; p. 53 Dustin Bradford/Getty Images; p. 56 Twin Design/Shutterstock.com; p. 57 YanLev/Shutterstock.com; p. 63 Africa Studio/Shutterstock.com; p. 65 Blend Images/Shutterstock.com; p. 67 dennizn/Shutterstock.com; p. 69 Mark Hunt/Hemera/Thinkstock; p. 74 pan_kung/Shutterstock.com; p. 83 Joseph Sohm/Shutterstock.com; p. 85 ID1974/Shutterstock.com; p. 89 Andre Luiz Moreira/Shutterstock.com; p. 92 shevtsovy/Shutterstock.com.

ABOUT THE AUTHOR

Jennifer Lombardo earned her BA in English from the University at Buffalo and still resides in Buffalo, New York. She has helped write a number of books for young adults, on topics ranging from world history to body image. In her spare time, she enjoys cross-stitching, hiking, and volunteering with local organizations.